Surprise!

Surprise!

The Secret to Customer Loyalty in the Service Sector

Vincent P. Magnini

BEP BUSINESS EXPERT PRESS

First published in 2015 by
Business Expert Press, LLC
222 East 46th Street, New York, NY 10017
www.businessexpertpress.com

ISBN-13: 978-1-63157-102-2 (paperback)
ISBN-13: 978-1-63157-103-9 (e-book)

Business Expert Press Marketing Strategy Collection

Collection ISSN: 2150-9654 (print)
Collection ISSN: 2150-9662 (electronic)

Cover and interior design by Exeter Premedia Services Private Ltd.,
Chennai, India

First edition: 2015

10 9 8 7 6 5 4 3 2 1

Printed in the United States of America.

Abstract

Modern consumers are bombarded with information from every angle. They can't handle it and, consequently, tune-out large portions of the information. Therefore, in order to gain their full attention, firms must find ways to surprise them during transactions—spawn mental script deviations for them. Research indicates that these script deviations can cement their loyalty. Therefore, *Surprise! The Secret to Customer Loyalty in the Service Sector* details how to create a surprise culture in a service firm.

Keywords

customer delight, customer service, customer surprise, services marketing

Contents

Acknowledgments

Special thanks to Ioana, Jim, Joel, Michelle, and Paul for offering feedback on early drafts of this book. Of course, very little is possible without the support of Olivia, Demi, and Michelle. Last, but not least, Molly's games of fetch were sometimes cut short due to this project: Molly, thank you for your unconditional support.

Introduction

The *good stuff…*

Some research is not worth the paper it is written on. It is ill-prepared and has no real implications for how we conduct business or live our lives. Some other research shapes our world and benefits us immensely. The good research helps us to live longer, be more productive, be happier, and have more fulfilling lives.

The trick lies in differentiating between the good and the bad.

In my roles as both a professor and a business consultant, I search for the valuable research findings. In doing so, the *good stuff* has been located that can improve how service businesses take care of their customers. *Any* service business can benefit from the message in this book: accounting to airline, entertainment to engineering, hotel to healthcare, landscaping to legal, pest control to plumbing, and restaurant to retail. In fact, even many firms that have traditionally been categorized as bearers of products would likely find this book useful as they gradually realize the importance of the service and experiential aspects of their business models. As we know, in recent years a number of companies such as IBM make greater profits with their service offerings than with their product offerings.

In this book, cutting-edge research is synthesized to deliver the following message: The volume of information going to your customers is at an all-time high and increasing. Your customers cannot handle this information overload, and tune-out most stimuli. Therefore, you must foster an organizational culture in which your firm continuously derives and implements new ways to surprise them. Not exceed their expectations, but surprise them—the difference will be demonstrated in these chapters.

Yes, you will find that the *good stuff* is compiled in this book for your use and enjoyment.

PART I

Your Customers Are Usually Not Paying Attention

Preview

Today consumers are bombarded with more commercially generated stimuli than ever before. Therefore, as your customers move through your business, they only pay full attention if there is a deviation from what they expect (a deviation from their mental scripts). Deviations can be triggered by service failures and can also be caused by delight initiatives that you choreograph. The heightened attention during these deviations should be used to cement loyalty.

CHAPTER 1

Information Overload

Introduction

This chapter details modern information overload and the responses that consumers are demonstrating.

For those of us old enough to remember, a given episode of *Murder She Wrote* had a beginning, middle, and an end. Angela Lansbury would encounter a scenario, the scenario would unfold, and the scenario would conclude.

The same held true for all of the former classics: *Matlock, Magnum PI, Leave it to Beaver, I Love Lucy, The Andy Griffith Show, Lassie, Laverne and Shirley, Happy Days, Welcome Back Kotter*, and so forth. In these sitcoms, there was one overarching story that commanded our attention. In modern years, however, a single TV show typically has numerous story lines intertwined, each competing for very small pieces of our attention. Such an evolution of television episode design is a reflection of a larger societal trend: Modern society bombards us with stimuli competing for small fractions of our awareness.

Competing for our awareness are also thousands of marketing messages each day. Ads pop up on our computer screens and are transmitted to us via e-mail, Twitter, and Facebook. Nearly every conceivable space contains a marketing message: Even the small 7 to 8 inch risers on the stairs exiting subway stations have ads printed on them. Marketing messages are stamped on egg shells as we cook breakfast; for example, CBS had its upcoming TV show line-up printed on egg shells. The recent recession coupled with the spike in gasoline prices caused many suburbanite commuters to sell advertising space on their cars. Ads are printed on T-shirts and hats and are even inked on the back of a bald man's head. Yes—in recent years there have been several incidents of bald men selling advertising space on their scalps. Women are now getting a piece of the action by leasing marketing space on their foreheads.

Modest-sized advertisements placed on public transportation buses are quickly going to the wayside—being replaced with bus wraps— advertisements that form a cocoon around the bus, competing for our attention.

The information overload is not limited to TV episode design and marketing messages, but can be evidenced in nearly every facet of society. It is estimated that more information was created in the final three decades of the 20th century than in the previous 5,000 years.[1] A weekly edition of the *New York Times* now contains more information than a typical person was likely exposed to in a lifetime in the 17th century.[2]

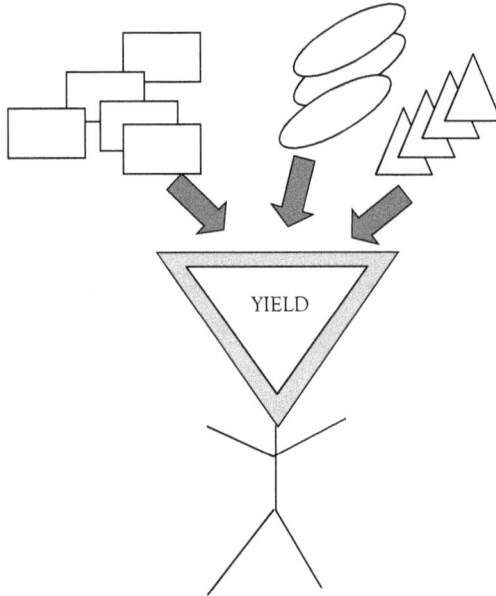

This information overload causes stress. For example, in a Reuters survey of business managers titled "Dying for Information," two-thirds of responding managers reported that they believe that information overload has damaged their personal relationships, and one-third believe that the overload has damaged their health.[3] We all know how it feels to be overwhelmed.

Feeling overwhelmed is stressful and being stressed is bad for our health. Well-known cardiothoracic surgeon, author, and television personality Dr. Mehmet Oz, posits that stress can be as detrimental to one's health as smoking cigarettes. According to Dr. Oz, stress can age our bodies up to 8 years, which is the same age estimation that he attributes, on average, to cigarette smoking—also 8 years. Although all sources and forms of stress are bad, according to Dr. Oz, the most damaging form is the constant nagging type such as the feeling of being overloaded. In his *New York Times* bestselling book titled *You: The Owner's Manual* he and his coauthor, Dr. Michael Roizen, state the following:

> Stress is the greatest ager of your body in general, especially the nagging, unfinished-tasks kinds of stress that hang over you day after day, or the stress of things that are out of your control (as opposed to the acute stresses—like having a flat tire or adjusting to a traffic jam when you are in a hurry—that eventually get fixed). We don't fully understand the mechanisms of how emotional stress produces physical stress, but we know it is a powerful connection.[4]

How do we respond to the stress spawned by the tsunami of information that bombards us each day? Albeit rude, the heavy flow of information primes us to multitask—consider, for instance, behaviors such as retrieving information from our mobile devices as we converse with others. Just look around a restaurant and watch diners use their mobile devices as they sit at tables with others. Research conducted at the Helsinki Institute of Information Technology finds that typical interfaces with mobile devices span between 4 and 8 seconds.[5] In short, we have become accustomed to fragmenting our attention. Even at the office, research shows that items occupy our attention on average for 3 minutes.[6]

Nevertheless, despite our ability to multitask, we often continue to feel bombarded and overloaded with information. We consequently (often unknowingly) develop defense mechanisms that block a large portion of such stimuli.[7] One coping mechanism, in particular, is called *satisficing*, which entails taking in just enough information to meet a need.[8]

Such satisficing applies to your customers as they move through your service environment. They have both consciously and subconsciously grown weary of the information overload that they continually experience and they purposefully take in just enough information to meet their goals in your service environment. In other words, your customers are sort of paying attention, but not really paying full attention so long as everything transpires according to what they expect.

Consider this, you are a customer at the counter in a sub shop and you are asked the following questions: What type of sub would you like? What type of bread would you like? Would you like a six inch or foot long? You then take three steps to the left and are asked: What type of cheese would you like? Would you like your sub toasted? You then take three more steps to the left and are asked: Which toppings would you like? You then take three more steps to the left and are asked: Would you like chips and a drink? In this scenario you are not paying attention because everything transpired according to your predefined script.

During a recent consulting project, a hotel front desk associate told me how she gives each guest checking-in a short introductory verbal narrative about the features and amenities of the hotel. As part of that narrative, she states that the breakfast restaurant is open daily from 6:30 a.m to 10:00 a.m. Many guests appear to be politely listening to her narrative, but, then, as they are leaving the front desk, ask her: Does the hotel serve breakfast?

A number of studies corroborate the notion that consumers do not actually pay attention when they are transacting in routine service exchanges. In fact, research identifies script theory, which posits that knowledge regarding familiar situations is stored in a consumer's mind as a coherent description of events expected to occur.[9] According to script theory, information about the service process is retained in a consumer's memory as a script (a sequence of actions that happen in a certain order).[10] Thus, customers in service encounters have well-formulated perceptions regarding their roles and regarding expected exchange characteristics. Consumers rely upon these perceptions and expectations and only truly pay attention when there is a deviation from the expected script.

Your customers rely on these scripts because the scripts reduce the burden of continually processing new stimuli.[11] Although reliance on scripts is heightened as a defense mechanism against modern information overload, the notion that humans use scripts (also known as schemas) to cope with incoming information dates back to the writings of Plato: "The world is complex, and yet people are able to make some sense out of it" and this is due, in part, to the use of scripts when perceiving one's surroundings.[12]

How are your customers' scripts formulated? Mental scripts of what they come to expect are derived primarily through their recollections of their previous transactions with your firm or in similar environments. If a particular customer is a new user in a service category, then a number of factors such as word-of-mouth and marketing messages contribute to script formation.[13]

Consumers' cognitive activities can be conceptualized as follows: (1) The stimuli are received (the customer is moving through our environment); (2) The customer asks herself: Is there already a mental interpretation (script) of this case; and (3) Do these new stimuli fit any of these previous interpretations (scripts) well?[14]

In fact, subconsciously, humans are so prone to compartmentalize new information into an existing script that errors are made in haste. Nobel prize winning psychologist and author, Daniel Kahneman, demonstrates that humans can perceive the letter B as being a 13 when it is positioned between 12 and 14.[15] In the 1930s, psychology researcher John Stroop found that asking individuals to state the word *blue* when it is written in red ink requires longer reaction times and yields more errors than if the ink color is congruent with the word being stated. These two cases help illustrate that consumers subconsciously work toward compartmentalizing incoming information into familiar scripts.[16]

Consequently, the only way to gain the full attention of your customers is to interject script deviations into their transactions. That is, to do something that they do not expect.

Key Takeaways

- Today's consumers are suffering from information overload.
- Information overload causes stress among consumers.
- In response to the stress stemming from information overload, consumers satisfice, which means that they only take in enough information to meet a need.
- Due to satisficing, as consumers move through service environments they only pay full attention when something transpires that they do not expect—that is a mental script deviation.

CHAPTER 2

Script Deviation

Introduction

This chapter explains how prompting script deviations (a.k.a. surprises) in consumers is different than exceeding their expectations.

A few years ago, a colleague and I conducted a study in which we analyzed the Internet blog postings written by those describing their experiences at particular hotels. We found something quite interesting: Nearly 100 percent of the consumers who typed the phrase *delightful surprise*, *excellent surprise*, *pleasant surprise*, or *positive surprise* in their blog postings indicated in the quantitative portion of the blog site that they would be willing to recommend the given hotel and would also be willing to stay there again.[1]

To restate the prior message: A positive script deviation yields almost guaranteed loyalty!

In this study, we then analyzed blog postings that used the word "delightful," "excellent," "pleasant," or "positive," but did not use the word "surprise." Of these consumers, only three out of four would affirmatively recommend or stay again at the described hotel. Not bad, but from a financial perspective, would you rather have a 75 percent customer retention rate or a 100 percent retention rate in your firm?

Next, we considered those blogs that used the phrase "very satisfied," but did not mention a surprise: in these, 60 percent would commit to recommending or repurchasing. This finding was interesting to us as well: if someone states that she or he is "very satisfied," wouldn't the retention rate be greater than 60? Not according to these results.

Finally, when a consumer used the word "satisfied" without "surprise," there was only a one-third likelihood that she or he would be a loyal advocate of the hotel. Again, the person writes in a blog posting that she or he is "satisfied," but despite this "satisfaction," two-thirds will not return.

The moral is evident: Surprises drive customers' reactions because that is when customers pay attention. In fact, service researchers term positive surprises as "customer delight." Specifically, research finds that *customer satisfaction* generally entails exceeding customers' expectations, whereas *customer delight* entails delivering a positive surprise beyond expectations.[2] Dr. Barry Berman, a marketing scholar, describes this distinction between customer satisfaction and customer delight in the following excerpt:

> Satisfaction is more cognitive; delight is more affective. Satisfaction is based on perceptions, while delight is more emotional. Delight is often associated with such emotions as arousal, joy, and surprise.... While satisfaction is based on meeting or exceeding expectations, delight requires out-of-the-ordinary experience.... Satisfaction is based on fulfilling the expected; delight is based on fulfilling unexpected positive surprise based occurrences. Satisfaction is based on meeting or slightly exceeding expectations, while delight occurs from features that are not expected or that add unexpected utility.[3]

On one occasion in my local bank, my attention was quickly attracted to the smell of donuts and freshly brewed coffee and a banner that read: "Our Goal is to Exceed Your Expectations!" I remember thinking that they could begin exceeding my expectations by taking down that ridiculous banner. "Exceeding Expectations" is perhaps one of the most commonly used and abused clichés in service businesses in recent years. It is likely that the popularity of the cliché stems from some very well-regarded and sound academic research that was conducted more than three decades ago. That is, in his research, a well—known and respected marketing scholar, Dr. Richard Oliver, advanced the notion that a consumer's satisfaction judgment in a service setting is a function of how the firm actually performs in comparison to what she or he expected.[4] According to the research, if a customer's actual experience matches his or her expectations, then a confirmation occurs. Or, if the actual experience falls short of expectations then a negative disconfirmation transpires, and the consumer is left unsatisfied. Lastly, if the actual experience exceeds expectations then a positive disconfirmation occurs, and the consumer is left satisfied.

This logic became known as the expectancy disconfirmation paradigm and has been widely accepted as the dominant conceptualization regarding how consumers formulate their satisfaction perceptions. In fact, Richard Oliver's 1980 article in the *Journal of Marketing Research* that details the expectancy disconfirmation paradigm has been cited in more than 6,000 other research articles. To offer some perspective, the average academic research article typically gets referenced by just one to two other articles. Like most, I find the expectancy disconfirmation paradigm to be quite useful and logical.

However, here's the issue: customer satisfaction (exceeding expectations) does have a connection with the customer's loyalty, but customer delight (a positive surprise) has a *much* stronger correlation with loyalty! Just consider the evidence from earlier in this chapter: Of the consumers who wrote in Internet blogs that they were satisfied, only one-third responded "yes" to the question of whether they would like to repurchase or recommend to a friend. Conversely, of the consumers who wrote in Internet blogs that they were positively surprised by something, nearly 100 percent answered "yes" to the question of whether they would like to repurchase or recommend to a friend.

As stated in Chapter 1, research spanning back several decades has documented this notion that customers do not actually pay full attention until something unexpected happens: This phenomenon is termed script theory. Because the surprise commands customers' full attention, it is much easier for you to connect with them on an emotional level. Delight is a more positive and more emotional response than being great or excellent; delight is an emotion-laden response that commits customers to an offering.[5,6]

Another unique feature of a script deviation is that the consumer's surprise reaction is immediate.[7] When a customer is surprised, you immediately have his or her attention. This immediate attention is there for you and your firm to capitalize on. On the contrary, satisfaction judgments based on expectancy disconfirmation evolve through time and are not immediate; hence, if you are merely satisfying by exceeding expectations, you are still competing with everything and everyone else that is trying to occupy a portion of the consumer's conscious thought.

From a physiological perspective, a lot happens in a person's brain when she or he is surprised.[8] First, the person appraises the unexpectedness by conducting a mental schema discrepancy check. The brain then redistributes some of its processing resources to make sense of the surprise event. Because of the heightened mental activity, it is actually an accurate statement when someone says that she or he *feels surprised.* That is, surprise can prompt a direct, sensation-like awareness.[9]

From a practical perspective, further evidence of the power of script deviations can be witnessed when your customers experience failures when transacting with your firm. Have you ever heard that it is often possible for your customers to be more highly satisfied with your firm after a failure and recovery with your firm than if the failure had never occurred in the first place? In other words, your customers' postfailure satisfaction levels exceed their prefailure satisfaction levels. Researchers coined the term "recovery paradox" to describe this effect. The recovery paradox was first discussed by a group of researchers in a *Harvard Business Review* article in 1990[10] and has since been validated by numerous studies.[11]

So your customers are more satisfied after you fail at something than they would be if you had never failed? At first glance, this logic seems to flunk the commonsense test. But, again, it relates to script theory; your customers are not paying full attention until they experience a script deviation: the failure is the script deviation. Because the failure serves as the script deviation, after the failure, you have the customer's full attention. If you then demonstrate an excellent recovery, the customer can experience satisfaction levels higher than prefailure levels.

In their 1990 game-changing *Harvard Business Review* article, Christopher Hart, James Heskett, and Earl Sasser used the story of a flight from New York to Cancun to describe the recovery paradox. The travel took 10 hours longer than scheduled, made two unplanned stops, ran out of food and drinks, circled 30 minutes before landing, and landed so rough that the oxygen masks dropped down. The general manager of the Club Med resort that the passengers were in route to heard of the travel problems and had set up a welcome station in the airport gate with soothing music, complimentary stress-reducing cocktails, and greeters to help with luggage. The satisfaction and loyalty of the travelers toward Club Med was likely much greater than if the travel problems had never occurred. In short, the travel problems prompted heightened attention due to script deviations and Club Med was able to capitalize on this heightened attention with kind gestures that went highly noticed.

The recovery paradox does not occur in all situations. The paradox will not transpire if the recovery is not well orchestrated. The paradox will also likely not occur if it is the customer's second failure with your firm. if they perceive that the failure was reasonably foreseeable or likely to occur again in the future. or if the failure was very severe.[12] But the principle holds: In most failure situations, it is possible to wow your customers because you have their full attention.

In fact, when you have their full attention after a failure, if you do not adequately resolve the situation, then a double deviation will occur. A double deviation can be described as a scenario in which failure recovery is so inadequate that the recovery is perceived by the customer as a second failure.[13] Therefore, once you have your customers' heightened attention, you must capitalize on the opportunity to impress!

To demonstrate this logic, we can use the example of the 2013 National Football League's (NFL) Super Bowl. During the second half of the 2013 game, there was a power outage in the stadium that halted game play for 34 minutes. Although the game and halftime show performances leading up to the power outage were well received, it was the outage that triggered a script deviation for the roughly 72,000 fans in attendance. It was during this time that some of the industry veterans seemed to display their understanding of the importance of capitalizing on script-deviating situations. Representatives from laundry detergent

Tide tweeted: "We can't get your #blackout, but we can get your stains out." Marketing reps from Oreo cookies tweeted: "Power out? No problem. You can still dunk in the dark." This Oreo tweet is said to have generated 16,000 retweets and 20,000 Facebook likes.[14] I wonder what percentage of the $3.8 million super bowl television commercials garnered 20,000 Facebook likes? Consider the return on investment (ROI) of those tweets.

The moral is that when unexpected things happen, people pay attention. If you are still not convinced of the power of script deviations, try this simple household experiment: the next time your significant other is sleeping, move his or her alarm clock from the side of the bed where it normally resides to the other side. Watch his or her reaction when it sounds in the morning. You will have his or her full attention.

Key Takeaways

- Script deviations (a.k.a. surprises) have a much stronger correlation with loyalty, positive word-of-mouth, and repurchase than does satisfaction.
- Customer surprises can also be termed "customer delight."
- Satisfying customers involves exceeding their expectations, but delighting them entails surprising them.
- Service failures are surprises that command the consumer's full attention and thus offer an opportunity to impress.

PART II

Surprise!

Preview

This section details how to create customer surprises that will trigger delight and loyalty. Customer surprises can come in many forms and can cost your business little or no money. A constant stream of new surprise ideas are needed for two reasons: (1) repeat customers can only be surprised once by a given tactic, and (2) your competitors will eventually copy your best ideas. Your firm's ability to generate and implement a steady flow of surprise tactics can serve as a sustainable competitive advantage.

CHAPTER 3

Stories From the Hotel Sector

Introduction

This chapter uses the hotel sector to illustrate how customer surprises can be incorporated into transactions.

Individuals continuously check whether their schemas match inputs coming from the surrounding environment. As soon as inputs diverge from the schema, surprise is elicited.
—Joelle Vanhamme and Dirk Snelders

With the advent of Internet booking sites, some argue that hotel rooms are at risk of becoming price-based commodities. Proactive hoteliers have been deriving strategies with mixed success to limit the commoditization of their offerings. The purpose of this chapter is to illustrate how surprise tactics can aid in this effort. The case of the hotel sector can be used to drive home the importance of consumer surprise.

Seven surprises in the first 17 hours:

- The family leaves their car in front of the hotel while they go to check-in. Upon completion at the registration desk, the father approaches the car to find a valet cleaning his windshield (Friday, 4:20 PM).

- The mother is taking the children from the lobby to their assigned room and sees that there is a wagon in the lobby that can be used to give the children a ride to the room in (Friday, 4:35 PM).
- As the family enters one of the hotel's restaurants for dinner, the hostess gives the children paper chef hats to wear (Friday, 6:15 PM).
- As the family waits for their food to arrive at the table, the children are given pizza dough to play with and mold on a paper plate (Friday, 6:40 PM).
- The father is interested in exploring the hotel's grounds and local area; he is told that there are free loaner bicycles in the hotel's lobby (Saturday, 7:35 AM).
- The mother and children are sleeping in the hotel room and they receive their scheduled wake-up call: the children are instructed to answer the telephone because the wake-up call is from their favorite animated cartoon character (Saturday, 8:00 AM).
- As the family walks down a hotel corridor to exit to go to an area amusement park, they see a housekeeping cart. With the parents' permission, the housekeeper then reaches into her cart and out emerges a bag of small toys, and each child is told that they can pick one (Saturday, 9:20 AM).

Cost: Seven surprises in the first 17 hours: approximately 70 cents:

- The family leaves their car in front of the hotel while they go to check-in. Upon completion at the registration desk, the father approaches the car to find a valet cleaning his windshield. **Approximate cost:** glass cleaner diluted in water = $0.03 per car.
- The mother is taking the children from the lobby to their assigned room and sees that there is a wagon in the lobby that can be used to give the children a ride to the room in. **Approximate cost:** price of wagon (and insurance) spread across 1 year of use = $0.03 per child.
- As the family enters one of the hotel's restaurants for dinner, the hostess gives the children paper chef hats to wear. **Approximate cost:** price of hat = $0.40 per child.

- As the family waits for their food to arrive at the table, the children are each given a piece of raw pizza dough to play with and mold on a paper plate. **Approximate cost:** dough and paper plate = $0.10 per child.
- The father is interested in exploring the hotel's grounds and local area; he is told that there are free loaner bicycles in the hotel's lobby. **Approximate cost:** price of bicycle spread over 3 years of use = $0.05 per guest.
- The mother and children are sleeping in the hotel room and they receive their scheduled wake-up call: the children are instructed to answer the telephone because the wake-up call is from their favorite animated cartoon character. **Approximate cost:** copyrighting permission = $0.05 per child.
- As the family walks down a hotel corridor to exit to go to an area amusement park, they see a housekeeping cart. With the parents' permission, the housekeeper then reaches into her cart and out emerges a bag of small toys, and each child is told that she or he can pick one. **Approximate cost:** price of toy = $0.07 per child.

Three surprises in the final 3 hours:

- As with the previous morning, on Sunday morning, the family is eating breakfast in the hotel's breakfast restaurant. The waitress remembers that the father requested tomato juice the previous morning, and without being prompted, asks him if he would like tomato juice again (Sunday, 8:40 AM).
- The family members are rolling their suitcases down the corridor because they are checking out. As they pass a housekeeping cart, the housekeeper thanks them for their business and asks them to return soon (Sunday, 10:15 AM).
- The father is checking out at the front desk. The front desk agent notices that he is wearing a Virginia Tech shirt and, therefore, proceeds to engage him in a short conversation about the upcoming Virginia Tech football season (Sunday, 10:50 AM).

Cost: Three surprises in the final 3 hours: free

Is it realistic to *assume* that it is possible to surprise customers with facets of customer service as previously described? This is actually not an *assumption*, but it is instead well documented that this can be the case. As described at the beginning of Chapter 2, a couple of years ago, a colleague and I conducted a study in which we analyzed the Internet blog postings written by those describing their experiences at particular hotels. When a consumer wrote the phrase "delightful surprise," "excellent surprise," "pleasant surprise," or "positive surprise" in their blog postings, we then read their postings further to identify what triggered these surprises. Of the nearly 800 blog postings reviewed, it was found that the most frequent (by far) trigger of these surprises was a facet of customer service. We routinely found that customers stated that they were surprised by how "friendly," "nice," "helpful," "pleasant," "accommodating," and "attentive" one or more staff members were in the transaction.[1]

How important is this finding? First, it illustrates that it is very possible to delight your customers with "free" facets of customer service. Second, as stated in Chapter 2, these customers who included a surprise phrase reported a nearly 100 percent willingness to recommend to a friend. Whereas, someone who used the phrase "very satisfied" without stating that she or he was surprised only reported a 75 percent positive word-of-mouth rate.

Even if the surprise idea costs money, another intention of this chapter is to use the case of the hotel sector to illustrate that the monetary cost need not be excessive. Once, when my daughters were younger, we were checking out of a hotel after a short family get-away weekend. At checkout, when we returned the two electronic key cards to the front desk agent, the agent asked my daughters if they would like to keep them as souvenirs. My daughters were delighted. During our first day back at our house they used the key cards to "play hotel" for the better part of an afternoon.

Several months later, I was helping one of my daughters to clean her bedroom when I found one of the key cards in a cabinet that she reserves for her "special" things—such as shells from the beach, notes from the tooth fairy, and so on. My daughters routinely asked my wife and me if we could return to that hotel ... and we did (several times). The key cards cost the hotel four cents each. That is a healthy ROI!

Is it more difficult to surprise an adult than a child with a low cost item? Truth be told, adults can be surprised just as easily; it is simply a matter of creativity. Approximately 2 years ago, for example, my family and I were staying at a hotel in Folly Beach, South Carolina, for a relative's wedding. My wife and daughters were members of the wedding party. After a late night rehearsal dinner, my family and I pulled up to the hotel tired and irritable. As we were exiting our car, the valet looked at me and asked: "How was the rehearsal dinner?" This was a script deviation for me. Of the hundreds of guests in the full hotel, how did he know that I was at a rehearsal dinner? Upon conversing with him, I found out that he had remembered helping me unload the three dress garment bags from my vehicle two days earlier. The fact that he paid enough attention to our interaction to remember a detail such as this made me feel special, like a guest in his house. So, yes, adults can just as easily be delighted by low or no cost surprise items.

Most of this chapter focuses on small things that hotels can do to trigger delight. What about the bigger things? For example, can the physical features of a hotel spawn positive surprises? Would guests be delighted by sculptures, architecture, or other visible atmospheric features within a hotel? The answer is "yes, but not very often." Such features are important for desired mood settings, but do not trigger surprises in hotels very often because now consumers can view detailed picture galleries and even take virtual tours of hotels before they arrive. Thus, it is rare that guests find these physical assets surprising during their experiences. Instead, service attributes and amenities must be strategically orchestrated to drive delight.

To illustrate the prior point, my family and I recently stayed in a hotel on the Canada side of Niagara Falls. We arranged for our room to have a "falls view." Were the falls beautiful to see from our room? Beautiful is an understatement; majestic, powerful, awe-inspiring might be more appropriate adjectives. In hindsight, are we glad that we paid extra to reserve a "falls view" room? Yes, we will always have this trip as a family memory. Did the "falls view" positively surprise us? Not really. When preparing for the trip, we went to "Google Images" and typed "Niagara Falls" and viewed the falls from every conceivable angle. Thus, the live view of the falls did not trigger a script deviation for us. The moral of this story is that even some of the most beautiful sites in the world will often not prompt script deviations—instead, other attributes in a service experience must surprise.

As detailed in Chapter 4, delight ideas can come in many forms. In the hotel coffee shop, for example, instead of issuing a guest loyalty card and punching one hole for the first purchase (five punches earns a free drink), rather punch three holes when the guest buys the first cup (seven punches earns a free drink). Punching three spots for one purchase positively surprises the guest, builds psychological momentum so that she or he will actually use the card, and, therefore, builds loyalty.[2] The key element is surprise! If the hotel doesn't have a coffee shop, the same concept applies to point-based reward systems—most hotels have point-based reward programs in which surprises can be infused. Again, creativity is needed in deriving surprise ideas.

Opportunities to surprise are endless. A group of college students were attending a conference at a hotel. One of the students sent out a tweet stating that she was at the conference. In her tweet she mentioned the name of the hotel. Almost immediately, a hotel associate picked up the tweet, contacted her, and asked if the hotel could do anything to make her stay special. Because she was a hospitality management student, a behind the scenes tour of the hotel was arranged. This example illustrates creative, inexpensive, and impactful delight.

This chapter concludes with a story of a slow-pitched, lobbed, softball right down the center of the plate that a hotel could have hit a grand slam with—but didn't even take a swing. This past March, a business consultant named Henry was driving to a speaking engagement when the area that he was driving through received a late season, poorly forecasted snow. As he was driving, the area received about three inches of snow that transitioned directly into freezing rain. The result was a highway that resembled the top of a 7-Eleven Slurpee—the driving surface was extremely slippery and there were accidents with a wide range of severity about every mile or so.

The stretch of the four-lane highway was rather rural with no real place to stop for food or shelter for about 20 to 25 miles. Once Henry could see civilization, he immediately pulled into the first hotel because he concluded that it would be too risky to venture any further until the

Opportunity!

next day. As he stood in line at the hotel's front desk, he realized that he was surrounded by other people who had not planned on staying at that hotel—they simply could not travel any further given the road conditions. As they waited to check-in, they exchanged horrifying stories of the near misses that they had avoided and the delays that they had experienced. Henry could see the stress on each person's face. These road conditions were a major script deviation for each person in the group—the danger commanded their full attention—they were all very cued-in to what was transpiring around them in this unintended hotel stop.

Because the hotel had their full attention, which is rare at hotel check-in, this would have been a great opportunity to delight. The agents could have offered words of comfort or empathy; a weather forecast for the next day; hot chocolate, hot tea, or coffee; a free room upgrade—anything to signal that they cared. Again, they had the group's full attention—so this was their opportunity to shine. Instead of shining, they stood in front of the hotel and smoked cigarettes once they checked everyone in.

Situations in which script deviations occur immediately before you begin transacting with your customers are golden opportunities—you have their full attention. Because we cannot bank on these all the time, we also need to know how to create script deviations. The next chapter, therefore, offers an array of strategies to employ in creating customer surprises.

Key Takeaways

- Surprise tactics can be creatively incorporated at many points throughout transactions.
- Surprise tactics can be implemented at little or no cost in service firms.

- Because a firm's physical features can often be viewed via the Internet in advance of transactions, it is almost always facets of customer service, as opposed to a firm's physical offerings, that surprise customers.

If a customer experiences a negative script deviation immediately preceding a transaction with a service firm, such a situation is an opportunity for the firm to impress because the firm has the customers' full attention.

CHAPTER 4

Surprises in Many Forms

Introduction

This chapter illustrates that surprise tactics can come in many forms.

Success is the sum of small efforts repeated day in and day out.
—Robert Collier

The previous chapter used the hotel sector to illustrate positive surprise opportunities. You might very well be thinking that it is easier to surprise a hotel guest than a guest in the sector in which you compete. After all, the window of surprise for a hotel guest often spawns 24 hours or more. The purpose of this chapter, therefore, is to demonstrate that surprise ideas are readily available in all service sectors.

There are endless ways of surprising customers in *any* service business: accounting to airline, entertainment to engineering, hotel to healthcare, landscaping to legal, pest control to plumbing, restaurant to retail. Surprising customers simply entails deriving innovative means of doing so.

To consistently surprise customers, a firm must be innovative. What is innovation? The term innovation is difficult to define. It is sometimes said that an innovation can be defined as something *new*. Although there is truth to this description, *new* is perhaps an even more difficult word to define: Can a firm's 2013 offering be described as *new*, or is it more appropriately described as an updated version of the 2012 offering? How is this distinction made?

When conducting management seminars in the area of innovation, I rely heavily on the following quote derived from Hungarian biochemist,

Albert Szent-Gyorgyi who won the 1937 Nobel Peace Prize for Medicine: "Discovery consists of seeing what everyone else has seen and thinking what no one else has thought." Thus, within the realm of service businesses, innovation entails seeing what everyone else sees in the business, but thinking something different. Because repeat customers can only be surprised once by a given item, and because your best surprise ideas will eventually be copied by your competitors, firms must be extremely innovative in deriving a constant flow of new ideas.

Surprising your customers can come in many forms. While the previous chapter described tangible and intangible items that were introduced to customers during points of interactions, this chapter focuses on alternative forms of service innovations.

First, the allocation of service tasks can be varied to spawn script deviations in consumers. For instance, consumers can be invited to participate in service tasks traditionally reserved only for the provider. Many of the hypothetical examples in the previous chapter involved a family with two children staying at a hotel. To continue along that path, suppose that the hotel in which the family was staying is nested within a resort environment containing an on-premise lake in which families can swim, rent boats, and fish. Thus, the family rents a boat and the kids catch a couple of fish. The resort could offer a program in which the kids could help the restaurant cook the fish as part of the family's dinner in the hotel's restaurant. Such experience cocreation heightens experiential qualities of the service exchange, fostering a bond (loyalty) between parties.[1] This cocreation experience opens the door to numerous other surprise opportunities: the kids are in the restaurant kitchen and can have their pictures taken with the chef, can help season the fish as they cook; can be given a tour of the kitchen; can be shown the walk-in refrigerator; and can be given chef hats.... In other words, cocreating facets of an experience that are traditionally not cocreated (traditionally produced solely by the provider) often allows for many surprise ideas to be interjected into the situation.

With regard to innovative ways of allocating service tasks to the consumer, rarely do you hear people say that they enjoy visiting doctors' offices. The most innovative medical networks now allocate some routine medical procedures to the patients to perform themselves at their homes. In other words, self-help capability is now being transferred to clients. If millions of diabetics can take their glucose readings at home, why can't many other routine procedures also be performed at home? As a result of this growing home-based health maintenance, the home healthcare industry has increased in size dramatically in recent years. Patients can perform routine tasks themselves and consult with home healthcare professionals when needed. Telling patients that they are not required to frequently return to the doctor's office triggers positive surprise in most. Most recently, at home "interactive" physical therapy tools have been designed to mimic video games such as Nintendo's Wii. Such devices aid home physical therapy programs by helping to ensure that individuals use proper form and technique when conducting rehab exercises in their homes.

Service tasks can also be reallocated among service providers to positively surprise customers. Suppose, for example, that you call a tree company because you had some storm damage to the trees at your residence. The tree company—very busy due to the high-occurrence damage from a recent storm—agrees to send a salesperson to view the damage and provide you with an estimated cost for the work. The salesperson subsequently arrives, tells you that the work is pretty basic and that if you agree to the price, he will not need to schedule for a crew to visit, but instead he has the gear to climb the trees and repair the damage while he is there that day. Or at a minimum, the salesperson performs enough work to alleviate immediate inconveniences such as impassable driveways. This immediate response pleasantly surprises you for several reasons: (1) the damaged trees are not only unsightly, but are also a safety hazard for those walking below; (2) you did not expect the salesperson to be cross-trained as a climbing arborist; and (3) the price is reasonable because the transportation and labor of an entire crew does not need to be arranged.

Although currently rare, in the airline sector, some airlines have the capability to train employees to check-in passengers through the use of a mobile device. It is quite surprising for travelers to enter into a long line and then be pleasantly surprised by one of the agents who approaches with a mobile device and executes the check-in. It is estimated that this practice can spawn delight for at least two or three more years until the practice becomes widespread to the point that it no longer surprises consumers.

In addition to the allocation of service tasks, customers can also be surprised by delivering service offerings in nontraditional locations. In retail banking, for example, first came ATMs and later online banking. The first banks to adopt these technologies delighted their customers through the convenience that such delivery modes provided.

Deriving novel delivery locations does not need to entail the implementation of new technologies. The first grocery stores, for instance, that offered free home delivery for out-of-stock items cemented patron loyalty. The cost of such service is low because individuals typically shop for groceries in their local neighborhoods. It is not an issue of cost, but rather an issue of innovativeness—deriving an idea before competitors. When an item is out of stock, this service failure serves as a script deviation—the customer is now paying attention—this allows the provider an opportunity to shine.

Here is a unique service innovation that involves delivery location: auto detailing services at movie theaters and shopping malls. While not yet commonplace in the United States, such services have done quite well in other locations around the world, particularly in Asia. In the Philippines, for example, moviegoers and shoppers can opt to have their vehicles washed (with a waterless system) and detailed while they enjoy a movie or shopping. After a movie or shopping outing, a family can enjoy a nice cinnamon or citrus-scented car for the ride home. Such innovative delivery location provides consumers with utility because they do not need to dedicate time to having their vehicles cleaned.

Furthermore, surprise can also come in the form of an unexpected price reduction. Picture yourself in an ice cream or frozen yogurt shop. You are absorbing all the delicate sugary sights and smells. You then receive your order and are paying at the counter so that you can extend your enjoyment to your taste buds. As you are paying, the attendant asks you: "Is it raining out right now?" You respond "yes." The attendant then says "well, in that case, you get a 25 percent rainy day price reduction." This is a significant script deviation because the store does not advertise this offering—the deal is announced at the point of sale. You won't be surprised next time you come for the rainy day discount, but it will certainly drive business on the lowest volume sales days—rainy ones.

An additional means of positively surprising service customers lies in altering the structure of the interaction. Even the most innovative hospitals—the ones that try and disguise their hospital identities with indoor waterfalls, abundant greenery, saltwater fish tanks, and modern food courts—have trouble putting patients at ease when the rubber meets the road: when it is time for the patient and doctor to interact.

A 2012 article in the *Harvard Business Review* details how this was successfully implemented in a healthcare setting.[2] That is, Club Red, a shared-medical appointment model, introduced at the University of Virginia Health System, significantly alters the structure of the traditional doctor's appointment. At Club Red, cardiac patients are offered a choice between the traditional one-on-one appointment or a 90-minute group appointment with as many as 11 other patients. Data reveal that patients value the group appointments: 98 percent satisfaction rating. In the group meetings, patients learn by listening to group dialogues concerning topics such as symptom diagnosis, lifestyle changes, and medication effects. Interestingly, Club Red members report a stronger rapport with the doctor because they witness his or her expertise in these group dialogues. Furthermore, the weight loss of group patients exceeds that of patients who opt for traditional appointments.

Evidently, some patients would probably prefer traditional one-on-one visits; therefore, optimal results would allow individuals to select the innovative or traditional structure. Nevertheless, the moral of this medical example is that customer delight can be spawned by innovatively altering traditional interaction structures. Moreover, the overarching message of this chapter is that service sector surprise ideas can take many forms.

Therefore, you should be creative in your surprise innovations. When discussing the topic of customer delight in a University course that I teach, a student recounted a story to me. After a morning of canoeing, he and his friends had worked up an appetite. They stopped for lunch at a restaurant and quickly consumed (inhaled) the food that they had ordered from the menu. The observant and motherly server then approached the table and asked "Would you like seconds?" Judging by the looks of confusion on their faces, the server explained that the restaurant was not busy at the moment and would be happy to prepare more food for them at no additional charge. They enjoyed a complimentary second course making them feel as if they were dining as guests in someone's house as opposed to in a restaurant. After all, isn't that what hospitality is all about? Making guests feel welcome.

When the student recounted this restaurant experience with me, I could still detect a sense of appreciation in his voice.

The thin profit margins that abound in the restaurant business do not make this tactic an appealing standard operating procedure, but it sure does fit well into a restaurateur's arsenal of surprise strategies.

The Walt Disney Company has an arsenal of surprise strategies. For example, Epcot delivers *unannounced* performances, including parades, magic shows, and character appearances. Unannounced is the key word because these tactics leave the guests being thankful that they happened to be in the right place at the right time. Disney's imagineers are some of the best in the world at deriving and orchestrating surprise strategies.

What if you cannot afford to employ designated imagineers at your firm? Successful customer surprise can be achieved by not only outspending your competitors, but instead by outthinking them. When it comes to surprise tactics, creativity can often be substituted for monetary spending. In his book the *Fred Factor*, business author Marc Sanborn, for example, details how a postal carrier named Fred continuously found ways to pleasantly surprise the homeowners on his route.[3] Fred's *official* job entailed placing mail in boxes—how creative can this get? Can a postal carrier really delight given the routine nature of the job position? Fred truly spent his career delighting his customers with unexpected things— taking their recycle bins out of the street, asking them how their trips were, writing personalized and thoughtful notes during the holidays, and so forth.

Again, it is not about outspending, but rather about outthinking. There is a devoted car salesman who keeps a handkerchief in his pocket so that he can wipe his customers' side view mirror as they pull away in their new car. It is a new car—how dirty can the mirror be? When asked about this gesture, I could hear passion in his voice. He explained that this is a gesture that delights because it is out-of-the-box thinking—who cleans a side view mirror with a handkerchief? It signals care, attention-to-detail, and costs nothing. The delight lies in the surprise and in the gesture itself.

To say it again, it is not about outspending, but rather about outthinking. There is a children's hospital in Russia where the window cleaners wear Spiderman costumes. When you get a chance, go to "Google Images" and search for "Spiderman window cleaner." You will see neat results of a firm that outthinks (rather than outspends) to trigger delight.

Have you ever wondered what happens to the flowers that go bad in a grocery store's floral department? They can likely be found around back in the dumpster. If a grocery store manager knows that she or he has an oversupply of a certain flower, how about giving them out from time-to-time in the check-out line? Spawning customer delight is about creativity.

Key Takeaways

- Surprise tactics can involve the reallocation of service tasks.
- Surprise tactics can entail delivering service in nontraditional locations.
- Surprise strategies can include unexpected price reductions.
- Surprise strategies can involve altering the structure of interactions.
- Even seemingly mundane services, such as mail delivery or window cleaning, can be infused with surprise tactics.
- Deriving successful surprise strategies does not depend on outspending competitors, but, instead, on outthinking them.

CHAPTER 5

Novel Surprise Ideas

Introduction

Because a patron can only be surprised by the same tactic one time, and because surprise ideas can be copied by competitors, this chapter reinforces the need for firms to derive a constant stream of new surprise tactics.

Surprising experienced customers entails choreographing many tactics

Chocolates on the Pillow Aren't Enough, is the title of a well-crafted book written by service industry veteran Jonathan Tisch and coauthor Karl Weber.[1] I completely agree that the practice of placing chocolates on hotel room pillows loses its surprise factor through time.

Suppose *customer A* is positively surprised by an amenity that she is offered during a visit to a local business. The next time that she visits the business, she is offered the same amenity and this time it does not trigger a surprise because she has already experienced it. Now there is no script deviation—no delight. She simply expects the amenity. For instance, perhaps you offer a customer free delivery on an appliance that she has ordered. When she places her subsequent order she might simply expect free delivery.

For that matter, many of the innovations detailed in the previous chapter will eventually cease to surprise repeat patrons. Group medical appointments, for example, will be surprising, script-breaking experiences at first, but sooner or later the novelty will fade for those long-timers.

To summarize the aforementioned scenario, from a practical point of view, there are two questions that need to be addressed: What if providing surprises raises the expectations of your repeat clientele? And, how do you surprise repeat customers?

To address the first question, there is little doubt that providing delight-filled surprise experiences will increase the expectations of your customers. There is also little doubt that it is increasingly difficult to surprise regular customers. The key to both of these issues resides in fostering an organizational culture rich in innovation in which dozens of new surprise ideas are continuously developed. Then, with a constant stream of new surprise ideas, the same customer can be repeatedly delighted.

In employing this strategy of rotating through surprise tactics, it is critical that a given idea is appreciated by a customer as something that is a pleasant, situation-specific gesture. In other words, the customer thinks: "I'm glad that I am in the right place at the right time." The situation-specific nature can be communicated during the delivery of the surprise. For instance, in reference to the scenario detailed at the beginning of this chapter, when the free delivery is granted during the first purchase it can be explained that it is not something that is normally offered, but rather something special that is being extended in this circumstance. In fact a 2013 study reported in the *Journal of Services Marketing* finds that the explanation that the service provider offers when delivering a surprise can go a long way in determining whether the customer will view the surprise as a "right time—right place" surprise or an expectation for each future transaction.[2]

It is not only vital to continually generate new surprise tactics so that regular customers can be repeatedly delighted, but also because such tactics cannot be patented. For the most innovative firms, by the time competitors have recognized and copied their surprise tactics, they have moved on to new ideas. The first couple of times that you cruise and see your cabin towels folded into animals it is pretty cool, but after that, the novelty fades. Furthermore, is there now a major cruise line company in the world that has not adopted the practice?

It is prudent to note, however, that some delightful ideas that meet specific criteria can be transitioned into routine deliverables. Such criteria include (1) low cost of delivery, (2) ease in implementing delivery on an ongoing basis, and (3) high value to the consumer. Once an item is transitioned into typical service delivery practices, its surprise triggering ability will diminish through time, but it can still foster satisfaction if it adds value to the consumer's experience. For instance, 30 years ago if a group of diners were to be offered free fortune cookies at the end of their meals this might have been surprising, but today it is commonplace.

Or, identifying a customer who calls you through the use of caller ID technology might surprise the customer in the first instance, but not in subsequent calls to your firm. Furthermore, if service providers in other sectors begin personalizing conversations through the use of caller ID, then your customer will also not be surprised when you do it as well. With surprise tactics, first mover advantage truly is an "advantage."

Creating a culture in which surprise ideas are generated in your firm before they are offered by competitors can serve as a formidable competitive advantage. In other words, it is not the ideas themselves that form your competitive advantage, but rather the culture that continuously generates the ideas. Former head of Shell Oil Company's strategic planning group was quoted as stating: "The ability to learn faster than your competitors may be the only sustainable competitive advantage." Cultures in organizations are not easily changed; therefore, if you can succeed in creating a culture in which you generate customer delight ideas before your competitors, then you could be the sustained leader in your competitive set.

In fact, a number of strategic management researchers have written extensively in recent decades about the *resource-based view* of the firm.[3,4] One of the fundamental components of the resource-based view is the notion that competitive advantages that are intangible in nature are often more sustainable than ones that are tangible. Aspects of corporate culture in a firm that can only be communicated throughout the organization through the passage of tacit knowledge—knowledge that cannot be readily communicated verbally or in writing, but rather is transferred through time—serve as the most sustainable competitive advantages. These intangible competitive advantages rooted in culture are those that are most difficult for competitors to duplicate. Although you cannot touch and feel such intangible assets of a firm, they can be quite valuable to a firm with regard to both short- and long-run success.

Grounded with the resource-based view logic, there is no question that a culture in which surprise ideas are consistently generated and implemented can be a formidable sustainable competitive advantage for a firm. Continuous generation and implementation of surprise tactics is certainly an intangible aspect of a firm's culture that is difficult to replicate. It requires that your team members possess the proper characteristics, that the relationships between them are marked with the proper traits, and that relationships with customers and other external constituencies are properly formulated.

If your team has the components necessary to innovate, a tool that they can use to help them hone-in on particular surprise ideas is service blueprinting. As discussed in my previous book, *Performance Enhancers: 20 Essential Habits for Service Businesses*, service blueprinting can be a very useful tool for deriving new surprise ideas in a service environment. In fact, it is a useful topic that received an entire chapter of attention in that previous book. Within the context of this current book, we briefly address it as a tool to identify surprise opportunities. Service blueprinting entails plotting diagrams of how individuals—both customers and employees— move through your business' physical environment. You then use those diagrams for a number of purposes, one of which being a means to derive surprise ideas for various points of contact. Many of the delight tactics listed in the hotel chapter (Chapter 3) were originally identified through the use of service blueprinting.

In many service businesses, the same points of contact will have different surprise potential depending on situational characteristics. For example, let us consider a hotel's front desk: surprise tactics will vary depending on travel occasion (e.g., business or leisure), check-in versus check-out, and even day of the week—people are often in different moods different days of the week. The point being raised here is that when you invest the time to develop blueprints, you should generate multiple copies so that you can use them to plot multiple situations to derive surprise ideas.

Last year, in a monthly newsletter sent to my consulting clients, I outlined some of the potential merits of service blueprinting. In response to the newsletter, the general manager of a very well-managed service business told me that they had actually made a number of copies of the architectural blueprints generated during a major facilities renovation and had used them to service blueprint for a number of years. His team would use the architectural diagrams of the physical spaces to derive ideas to better serve their customers. Pretty smart.

Even with tools such as blueprinting available, your employees need to be motivated to surprise. Thus, the next section of the book details the organizational components needed to foster a culture in which a steady stream of innovative surprise ideas is the norm. When a competitor steals a surprise idea, that is OK, you have already moved on to the next one.

In some sectors, such as in retailing, surprise ideas circulate pretty rapidly between competitors. In other sectors, surprise ideas are few and far between; for example, when was the last time that you were surprised by a movie theater employees' surprise tactic? Or, at a car oil-change facility? Or, at a library (for that matter, by any government employee)? Regardless of your sector, competitive advantage is derived from generating and implementing the best script-deviating ideas first.

In a classic *Harvard Business Review* article titled "Welcome to the Experience Economy" authors Joseph Pine and James Gilmore offer firms some sound advice: "Companies should think about what they would do differently if they charged admission."[5] In other words, in order to derive the best surprise ideas (before competitors) your mental model should not be "delivering services" but rather "staging experiences."

Key Takeaways

- Because a patron can only be surprised by a given tactic one time, deriving a steady stream of surprise ideas should be engrained into a firm's corporate culture.
- Deriving a steady stream of surprise ideas should also be a facet of a firm's corporate culture because surprise ideas cannot be patented and will be copied by competitors.
- Practicing service blueprinting will help a firm derive novel surprise ideas.
- To foster innovation, the guiding paradigm in a service firm should be about "staging experiences" as opposed to "designing services."

PART III

Generating Surprise Ideas: An Employee's Perspective

Preview

Generating a continuous stream of surprise ideas requires a culture founded upon innovation. First and foremost, people on your team must be motivated to innovate and have the ability to do so. Regarding motivation, your employees are most innovative when they are satisfied with their jobs. In terms of ability, you can screen for creativity in your hiring process, but must also screen for emotional intelligence and a learning orientation because an individual's creativity cannot be manifested in your firm without these other two characteristics. Furthermore, in order for your firm to be innovative, those on your team must be aware of each others' areas of expertise and must also feel that they have access to each others' expertise.

CHAPTER 6

Employees' Motivation to Surprise

Introduction

This chapter details how to motivate frontline surprises and how to formulate and implement customer surprise tactics.

> Why did the kid throw the butter out of the window?
> (To see the butter fly.)
>
> What color socks do bears wear?
> (They don't wear socks, they have bear feet!)
>
> Where does a 500-pound canary sit?
> (Anywhere it wants!)
>
> What's yellow, weighs 1,000 pounds, and sings?
> (Two 500 pound canaries!)[1]

Typing "jokes and riddles for kids" in the Google search engine will produce websites containing lists of such jokes and riddles. If your employees interact with kids in a movie theater, in a restaurant, on a train, or on an airplane would it not be advantageous if they knew a few such riddles to surprise kids, with humor? Evidently, the answer is "yes," but your employees must be motivated to use the Internet to build their riddle arsenals.

Business author James Donnelly wrote: "We must never forget that service businesses do not produce—they perform. They do not sell *things*—they sell human performances."[2] The actors—your employees—are, therefore, at the heart of delivering customer delight. Your success hinges upon their performance.

If you recall, Chapter 3 concluded with a story about employees who had a golden opportunity to delight at a hotel during a snow and ice storm. Instead they opted to quickly conduct routine transactions with customers and then congregate to smoke cigarettes. What caused the employees to behave at such a subpar level? The answer lies with either their motivation or their ability—and, in some cases, it is both.

The generation of a constant stream of customer surprise ideas by your employees depends on their motivation and their ability to derive and implement these ideas. This chapter addresses motivation that is driven largely by employee job satisfaction. Your employees' levels of job satisfaction have a significant influence on their innovativeness.

Recently, for example, a forward-thinking manager told me that he encourages each of his employees to do at least one thing per day to surprise a customer. The surprise could come in the form of remembering that the customer likes green tea or personalizing a conversation. The manager understands the importance of script deviations and attempts, day-in and day-out, to communicate the importance to his staff. The fact is that there are numerous ways in which guests can be surprised. Employees, however, will not be motivated to derive and display these surprise ideas if they do not like their jobs. Studies dating back more than 3 decades find that the generation of innovative ideas depends on one's motivation to engage in such mental processes.[3,4]

The linkage between job satisfaction and innovativeness is largely driven by the fact that innovation in organizations requires that employees share knowledge and ideas; an individual's job satisfaction impacts his or her willingness to share knowledge with coworkers.[5] Poor job satisfaction not only impedes knowledge outflow, but also your employees' motivation to collect knowledge from coworkers that can be used to bolster innovation.[6] It boils down to organizational commitment: if employees are not happy, then they are likely not committed; therefore, they have little motivation to further innovate.[7]

Is the research described in the previous paragraph accurate? If your employees are not satisfied, will this significantly influence their motivation to derive surprise ideas? At first glance, this logic is questionable because no one wants to perform poorly at their job. Doing a job well provides an inner satisfaction as well as a social identity in the workplace. In his book *The Fred Factor*, Marc Sanborn succinctly writes:

> One thing seems common to all human beings: a passion for significance. I've never met anyone who wanted to be insignificant. Everyone wants to count, to know that what he or she does each day isn't simply a means of making a living, but a "living of making a meaning."[8]

Here's the catch: even if your employees attempt to perform at a high level when their satisfaction is low, they have trouble achieving the high levels due to their lack of satisfaction. That is, research indicates that even if your employees do not intend to perform at a lower level, poor satisfaction can cause them to do so subconsciously. Here is an illustration of how one's satisfaction can influence behavior on a subconscious level: A number of years ago in Israel, a parole judge would be assigned to determine whether or not a prisoner was fit to rejoin society. The judge would review the parole file, which took an average of 6 minutes and then decide whether the application should be accepted or rejected. The overall approval rate was 35 percent. The judge would stamp his or her decision on the file along with the date and time that the decision was made. Interestingly, when these stampings were analyzed, it was found that, on most days, the judge would approve almost no cases that were analyzed within a short time before a meal break. Conversely, the acceptance rate would spike to near 65 percent when considered after a meal break.[9] The message is clear: even in processes that are intended to be unbiased, we are humans, therefore, our satisfaction affects our decisions. So, yes, your employees' satisfaction does influence their innovativeness both consciously and subconsciously. That's human nature.

As we know, keeping our employees satisfied and motivated is both an art and science and often does not come easily. Former New York Yankees baseball manager, Casey Stengel, was quoted as saying: "The secret of managing is to keep the five guys who hate you away from the guys who are undecided." Evidently, it is unrealistic to expect to present some sort of magic formula in this chapter regarding how to keep employees satisfied. It is, however, possible to outline some of the key research findings on the topic.

While the job satisfaction of your employees is driven by many contextual factors, the primary determinants of job satisfaction in any domain are their perceived levels of justice: distributive justice, procedural justice, and interactional justice. If your employees feel that these three forms of justice are high, then they will be satisfied with their jobs.

Distributive justice pertains to whether your employees perceive that the company's resources are being allocated fairly.[10] Do they feel that they have fair compensation? Do they feel that the most deserving candidate received the promotion? Do they feel that their benefits packages are fair? Do they feel that the pay raises associated with their performance evaluation are adequate representations of their performance?

Next, your employees' perceptions of procedural justice involves whether they feel that the company's procedures are fair.[11] A key driver of procedural justice perceptions is communication. Often employees will view a procedure or policy as being unfair because they have never been told the rationale behind the policy. Not always, but often, once they understand why the policy is in place, then procedural justice perceptions improve.

Interactional justice entails whether your employees perceive their interactions with you and other managers as respectful.[12] That is, do they perceive you as being rude or cooperative? Are you viewed as a good listener or close-minded and arrogant? A key driver of interactional justice perceptions are the manager's listening skills. You evidently do not need to agree with everything that your employees say, but you should demonstrate that you are listening. For example, when I conduct training sessions for service employees, I stand at the door of the training room and greet the employees as they enter. Sometimes the business manager stands with me to help greet. A wide range of manager skill levels can be witnessed during this greeting process. Some do not even address their employees by their names. The best managers, on the other hand, use the opportunity to demonstrate their listening skills. As employees enter, they make comments and ask questions to demonstrate that they listen: "How's your new grand baby?" "How was your son's soccer game?" "How do you like your new car?" "How was your family reunion?," and so forth.

To summarize, if you want your employees to be motivated to generate and implement customer surprise tactics, then they need to be satisfied with their jobs. Job satisfaction is a function of their distributive, procedural, and interactional justice perceptions. One item that has a significant impact on all three forms of justice is the feedback that you give to your employees. We all love feedback—the more the better. If you see them doing something well, tell them. If something can be done better, tell them. Kenneth Blanchard and Spencer Johnson's national bestselling book *The One Minute Manager* really drives home the importance of feedback. Although the message is more than 30 years old, it is still critical in shaping the job satisfaction of our employees.[13] Most people do not realize that receiving no feedback is typically much more demotivating than receiving constructive feedback. No feedback minimizes the employee's role as one that is not even worthy of the adequate attention to where delivering feedback is even worthwhile. In other words, no feedback sends the following message: "Your role is not worthy of my attention."

Interestingly, a recursive cycle can be conceptualized in which employee satisfaction leads to the generation of customer surprise ideas and carrying out the surprise ideas then contributes to employee satisfaction. This loop is conceptualized because it feels good to satisfy customers. A recent book authored by University of Pennsylvania business professor, Dr. Adam Grant, titled *Give and Take* details much research illuminating how it is often much more satisfying for humans to give than to receive.[14] In service delivery, the provider can be conceptualized as the giver. Therefore, deriving ideas that pleasantly surprise customers during their transactions with the firm is typically found to be intrinsically rewarding. It feels good to deliver (*to give*) customers enjoyable experiences.

To further elaborate, a recursive cycle is conceptualized because emotions are contagious and customer satisfaction has a mirror effect with employee satisfaction.[15] Because customers and employees interact, their moods and emotions also interact. Anchored in the field of social

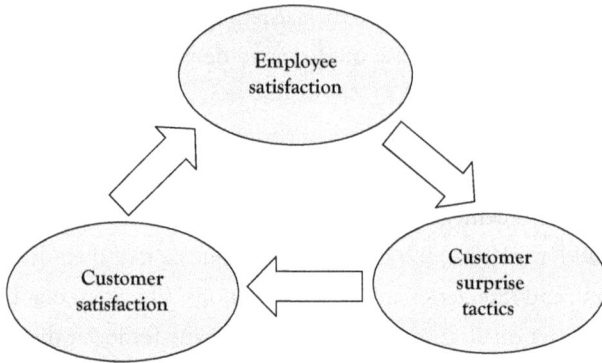

psychology, emotional contagion theory explains an individual's tendency (even subconsciously) to align his or her behavior with that of others in order to converge emotionally.[16] Thus, while job satisfaction can help spawn creative delight ideas, the delight ideas can then loop back into employee satisfaction.

There is one company in particular in the service sector that has a reputation for creating a culture in which employees routinely go out of their way to pleasantly surprise customers with small gestures. I happen to know an executive in that organization. When I asked him how the company motivates its employees to derive and implement delight ideas on a daily basis, the first few responses that he gave me were somewhat shallow ideas likely practiced by most service firms—he was being fairly tight lipped. After probing a little deeper, however, he divulged a practice that can be quite impactful. He told me that during the employees' daily shift meetings, someone in the meeting must tell a story of how a customer was positively surprised within the last few days. This component of the shift meeting creates a culture centered upon delight, motivates the employees to delight, and creates a forum in which they can exchange delight ideas. This practice is powerful.

Lastly, your employees will not be motivated to surprise customers unless they *all* understand why it is important to surprise customers. The logic contained in this book needs to be explained to them. Communicating this message should begin in employee orientation and should continue to be clearly articulated throughout the duration of employment. They truly need to buy into the fact that script deviations lead to loyalty and associated behaviors such as repurchase and positive word-of-mouth. In today's information age, surprise is a key component of top-rate service delivery; it is needed to garner attention.

Key Takeaways

- An employee's job satisfaction is positively correlated with his or her innovativeness in deriving and carrying out customer surprise tactics.
- An employee's job satisfaction is driven by his or her perceptions of the firm's distributive, procedural, and interactional justice dimensions.
- The quality and quantity of feedback provided by the manager to the frontline worker impacts all three forms of justice perceptions.
- Requiring employees to share customer surprise stories in daily shift huddles helps motivate them to formulate and implement surprise strategies.

CHAPTER 7

Employees' Ability to Surprise

Introduction

This chapter outlines how there are certain characteristics that a front-line employee needs in order to possess the capability of deriving and implementing customer surprise tactics.

To foster a culture within your organization in which innovative surprise ideas germinate routinely, you need to hire employees who are creative.

Occasionally, vehement job applicants will demonstrate their creativity without being prompted to do so. The hypercompetitive job market triggered by the recent recession prompted some individuals seeking employment to take measures to stand out in the application process. Colorful office water cooler stories include tales of applicants that submit interactive videos in their application materials, include a Pinterest link, or send the hiring team a Lego model with a description of its significance. Stories can also be heard of applicants who include humorous letters of endorsement from their mothers. For example, one such letter read: Please hire my son. He is a nice boy. He is kind to others and very smart as well. He has outstanding personal hygiene. I taught him to wear clean underwear; and [as far as I am aware] he hasn't wet his bed in nearly 20 years....

While such unsolicited displays of creativity can demonstrate outside-the-box thinking, how can you assess the creative potential of all key applicants? That is, when you are hiring new employees, what measures do you have in place to assess their creative ability? Because a firm is a collection of individuals, it stands to reason that the more creative each of the individuals, the more likely the firm is to be innovative. For this reason, many firms incorporate one or more creativity tests as part of their selection procedures.

As detailed in Malcolm Gladwell's bestselling book, *Outliers*, here's one such creativity test[1]: In the next four minutes, write down as many uses that you can think of for the following objects:

1. A brick
2. A blanket

Applicant A:

(Brick) To break a window. To build a house. To make a toilet more environmentally friendly. To make a walk-way. To decorate. To throw. A paperweight. To build a chimney. To make a pizza-oven. To smash. To hammer. To drill. A doorstopper.

(Blanket) To cover up with when sleeping. As a tent. To send smoke signals. To use on an airplane. As a sail. To dry your hands. To cover your naked body. Make sex more comfortable. To catch people as they jump out of a building. For a picnic. Use as a target for shooting practice. To wrap furniture when moving. To embroider.

Applicant B:

(Brick) To build a house. To weigh things down.
(Blanket) For keeping warm. For covering up with.

Given the aforementioned responses, would you say that Applicant A or Applicant B is more creative? The answer is obvious. This divergence test is a simple assessment of creativity that is free to use, is simple, and is, therefore, ripe for adoption by any firm regardless of size.

Other than this brick–blanket divergence test, there are quite a few creativity tests available for use by firms; several have been available for a number of years. Perhaps the best-known of the tests are the Torrance

Tests of Creative Thinking (TTCT), initially published in 1966 and since revised several times.[2] TTCT ask that examinees recollect upon their past experiences. TTCT then prompts examinees to draw and give a title to their drawings or to craft questions, reasons, consequences, and different uses for objects. Scoring of these tasks is often done using three scales:

- Fluency—how many meaningful ideas are generated in response to the stimuli?
- Originality—how rare are the given responses?
- Elaboration—how much detail is contained in the responses?

These three evaluative criteria relate directly to surprise creativity. The goal is to hire individuals who derive numerous surprise ideas (fluency), generate ideas that are rare in a given industry (originality) and ideas that can be detailed enough to successfully implement in a dynamic operation (elaboration).

If you are a small firm and you do not feel comfortable utilizing paper and pencil creativity tests—doing so simply does not fit into your business model or culture—there are some other very simple ways of assessing creativity. For example, if your firm opts not to use defined tests such as TTCT, screening for creativity can be achieved by asking a candidate to provide a solution(s) to a challenge that confronts the firm. For instance, an internship application for a large hotel once asked one of my students to write a paragraph detailing a creative way to reduce guests' perceived waiting times at check-in. Just think about the many surprise opportunities that present themselves at guest check-in—it is a blank surprise canvas. Creativity can be assessed by soliciting such paragraphs from all applicants. If an applicant is given a few days or longer to offer a well-formulated solution to an issue, but fails to exhibit a creative response, then it is unlikely that the individual will demonstrate creativity if hired.

All firms, regardless of size, can insert a couple of verbal questions into their interviewing that assess creativity. It is well documented that particular behavioral interviewing questions can help elicit candidates' creative ability; the following are some examples from Victoria Hoevemeyer's book, *High Impact Interview Questions*[3]:

- A lot of times, we use tried-and-true solutions to solve problems, and it works. Tell me about a time when the tried-and-true solution did not work. Were you able to solve the problem? How?
- Tell me about a situation in which you have had to come up with several new ideas in a hurry. Were they accepted? Were they successful?
- Tell me about a time when you created a new process or program that was considered risky.

While you are at it, you may also be well-served to ask the candidate how she or he has delivered innovative service at a previous workplace. How was the idea derived? Did it work well? What were some of the challenges associated with the surprise strategy? What was the customer's reaction? How can the idea be improved or updated for future implementation?

Creative individuals possess a capacity for divergent thinking, which entails originality, fluency of ideas, flexibility, and the capability to elaborate and refine.[4] Research focusing on individual creativity often explores specific traits that distinguish creative from noncreative individuals.[5,6] A number of studies also focus on the process that individuals utilize in generating creative ideas.[7,8] For example, creative people are said to have the ability to connect disparate sources of information, which serve as the foundation for new ideas.[9-11] In other words, they possess the ability to migrate ideas from one context to another.[12] Such migration is needed in order to adapt surprise ideas from competitors and, more importantly, from outside one's industry. Therefore, if you ask a job candidate one or more of the previous questions, one of the elements that you are seeking in the answer is the adaption of ideas and processes into contexts in which they have yet to be applied. For example, if a job candidate discusses how she or he worked at a country club and implemented ideas from a theme park experience—this would be an outstanding response.

It is also prudent to note that the overall reputation or image of a firm can help (or hinder) the draw of creative talent. Some firms, such as Google, tend to attract highly creative applicants through an image that they have in the marketplace. Many firms use tools such as YouTube, Facebook, and Twitter to help shape such an image. Companies have images and personalities just as people do. They can be creativity magnets, the same way that the cool kids in high school can attract cool friends. For example, a firm that is thought of as being "daring" or "trendy" would likely attract a more creative applicant pool than one that is perceived as being "traditional" or "rigid."

When attempting to draw creative individuals for employment, the nature in which the job posting is written can make a difference. A boring position announcement—communicates a boring position—and attracts boring applicants. In your firm, maybe your marketing team should help your human resources team write the position descriptions? Often the marketing department's ability to communicate a certain image in written text surpasses the ability of the HR folks. The culture of the firm should come through in the posting: "…if you join our team, your dry cleaner will not be happy; we want you to wear clothes in which you are relaxed and even wear flip flops in the summer (all six weeks of it)…." Perhaps the HR team can craft postings such as this, but they should stop calling themselves HR and begin calling themselves talent managers—much more creative. What if you do not have a HR team and a marketing team? The point is that your position announcements need to be crafted well in order to attract the best talent. Thus, take your time when writing the descriptions; see how the positions of your competitors are written; and if you are not a skilled writer then find a colleague to help you write your position announcements.

Although it is recommended that you assess applicants' creativity in your selection process, the usefulness of such creativity assessments has been called into question in the academic literature.[13,14] That is, it is unclear whether the use of such creativity testing has a significant influence on a firm's innovativeness. Because, conceptually, a firm is a collection of individuals, it seems plausible that a group of more creative people would yield a higher level of innovation than a group of less creative people. But, again, evidence that creativity tests yield firm innovation is mixed.

Studies measuring the usefulness of creativity tests show mixed results because in a work setting, individuals need to implement their ideas in a group context—the tests do not typically measure the capacity to interact in a group. In other words, creativity assessment in the selection process falls short of gauging whether an individual would have the ability to successfully implement the creative ideas in an organization. In order for a creative person to implement his or her ideas in your organization, she or he will need a learning orientation and a high level of emotional intelligence. That is, Johnny might be creative, but such creativity is wasted if he is scared of sharing his creative ideas with his work team.

A leaning goal orientation (referred to in this book as a "learning orientation") is one of two goal orientations identified in research conducted by Stanford psychology professor Carol Dweck and her colleagues[15–17] and later validated by a number of other researchers.[18,19] Some individuals exhibit a learning orientation in which they have a preference to develop one's competence by acquiring new skills and mastering new situations.[20] Conversely, other individuals tend to possess a performance goal orientation in which they have a preference to demonstrate and validate one's competence by seeking favorable judgments from others.[21] For example, when a performance goal-oriented person completes a task in which results are poor or ambiguous, the individual would tend to avoid that task in the future. A person with a learning orientation, on the other hand, would desire to attempt the task again with a revised strategy.[22]

Within the context of this chapter, it is posited that a person identified as being highly creative in a creativity test would need a learning orientation in order to transform creative ideas into firm innovation. An individual within an organization would need to be "thick-skinned" and not fearful of failure in order to present novel ideas to his or her work team. Thus, as depicted in the following figure, it is proposed that an individual's learning orientation intervenes in the relationship between his or her creativity and firm innovation.

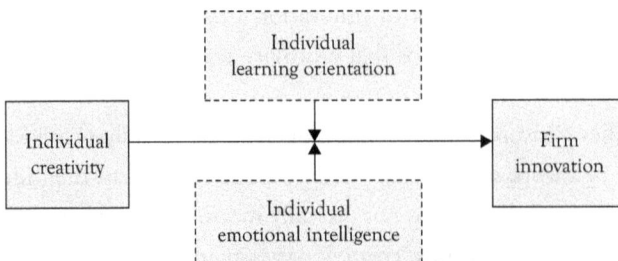

Just as creativity is assessed in the hiring process, so should a candidate's learning orientation be assessed. If a survey is desired, the following figure provides survey questions that can be used for this purpose. These survey questions were developed by learning orientation researchers in the 1990s and remain valid for today's use.[23,24] A seven-point Likert-type scale that ranges from strongly disagree (1) to strongly agree (7) is applicable to these survey items. A higher average score on the "high learning orientation" statements than on the "low learning orientation" statements is an indicator that the candidate is learning oriented

Low learning orientation:

I prefer to do things that I can do well rather than things that I do poorly.

I'm happiest at work when I perform tasks on which I know that I won't make any errors.

The things that I enjoy the most are the things that I do the best.

The opinions others have about how well I can do certain things are important to me.

I feel smart when I do something without making any mistakes.

I like to be fairly confident that I can successfully perform any task before I attempt it.

I like to work on tasks that I have done well in the past.

I feel smart when I do something better than most other people.

I feel that there aren't a lot of new things to learn about my line of work.

I spend a lot of time thinking about how my performance compares with that of other managers.

I always try to communicate my achievements to the corporate office.

I feel very good when I have outperformed other managers in my company.

It is very important that the corporate office sees me as a good manager.

High learning orientation:

> The opportunity to do challenging work is important to me.
>
> When I fail to complete a difficult task, I plan to try harder the next time that I work on it.
>
> I prefer to work on tasks that force me to learn new things.
>
> The opportunity to learn new things is important to me.
>
> I do my best when I work on a fairly difficult task.
>
> I try hard to improve on my past experience.
>
> The opportunity to extend the range of my ability is important to me.
>
> When I have difficulty solving a problem, I enjoy trying different approaches to see which one will work.
>
> It is worth spending a lot of time learning new approaches for dealing with job challenges.
>
> An important part to me being a manager is continually improving my management skills.
>
> I put a great deal of effort in order to learn something new about managing.
>
> It is important for me to learn from every management experience that I have.
>
> Learning how to be a better manager is of fundamental importance to me.

If you are a small firm and do not wish to administer surveys during the hiring process, a candidate's learning orientation can also be assessed through the use of particular behavioral interviewing questions. Any questions that you craft asking a candidate to describe his or her comfort with unfamiliar situations would work just fine in this effort; for example: "Describe a time when you tried to accomplish something and failed." Responses to such questions can provide insights into an individual's learning orientation. When evaluating responses to such items you are looking for indications that candidates see ambiguous situations and even failures as learning opportunities for future development.

Because a firm consists of a collection of individuals, it is also posited that a person identified in testing as being highly creative would need to be emotionally intelligent in order for that creativity to make a difference with regard to firm innovation. Presenting a novel (creative) concept to a group of colleagues with the goal of soliciting their buy-in so that the concept can be implemented requires emotional regulation and proper emotional channeling. Therefore, an individual's emotional intelligence also intervenes in the relationship between creativity and firm innovation.

The concept of emotional intelligence was popularized by two well-known researchers, Peter Salovey and John Mayer at Yale University and the University of New Hampshire, respectively, as a type of social intelligence that is distinct from general intelligence.[25] In their initial writings, they described it as "the ability to monitor one's own and others' feelings and emotions, to discriminate among them, and to use this information to guide one's thinking and actions."[26] This conceptualization of emotional intelligence was subsequently extended to encompass the capability of a person to accurately perceive, appraise, and express emotion; the capability to access and produce feelings when they facilitate thought; the ability to comprehend emotions; and the ability to monitor emotions to stimulate emotional and intellectual development.[27]

Like creativity, a candidate's emotional intelligence can also be assessed in the selection process. If a survey mechanism is desired, there are dozens of surveys that can be found on the Internet designed to assess an individual's emotional intelligence. For example, the seminal emotional intelligence researchers, Salovey and Mayer, developed a 24-item survey that measures six dimensions: self-encouragement, social skill, smooth interpersonal relationship, praising others, self-emotion management, and observation of other's feelings. Such surveys administered in the selection process help build a tentative picture of a candidate's level of emotional intelligence.

With regard to interviewing, emotional intelligence can also be gauged by observing a candidate's reactions to multiple interviews, group interviews, or being interviewed by line-level workers. Multiple interviews can assess if the candidate's demeanor is consistent at multiple points in time. Group interviews can assess if the candidate is able to manifest his or her personality and emotions well when interacting in a group setting. And, being interviewed by future subordinates gauging his or her demeanor in this context—is she or he able to establish rapport with the subordinates or does she or he come across as being condescending?

Unique and varied past experiences on the applicants' resume can also be a potential signal of both a learning orientation and emotional intelligence. For example, if a candidate has worked as an expatriate in another country then the candidate has likely developed what is termed *acquired diversity*, which is developed through experience. This is distinct from *inherent diversity*, which stems from traits with which someone is born. Recent research finds that acquired diversity has a stronger link to firm innovativeness than inherent diversity.[28]

To summarize the earlier discussions, this chapter contends that firms should use employee creativity testing in the selection process, but should also consider mechanisms to assess a candidate's learning orientation and emotional intelligence. Learning orientation and emotional intelligence are essential "keys" for unlocking creativity. A creative person needs a learning orientation in order to feel comfortable bringing forward his or her creative ideas within the organization. Likewise, a creative individual needs to be able to effectively manage his or her emotions, read the emotions of others, and manage interpersonal relationships in order to implement his or her creative ideas within your organization.

From a managerial perspective, it is germane to note that it is not always possible to find an ideal job candidate that meets all of the employment criteria including high creativity, learning orientation, and emotional intelligence scores. Furthermore, it is well recognized that these three characteristics may not be the most pressing characteristics that you are seeking in a candidate. For example, if you are a tree service company hiring a new salesperson, yes, creativity, a learning orientation, and emotional intelligence would be nice, but the most important attributes are knowledge of trees and tree work, punctuality, and salesmanship. Thus, it is important to recognize that even if you do not screen for all of these characteristics in the hiring process, some can be developed once a person is hired. Specifically, research indicates that both a learning orientation[29,30] and emotional intelligence[31,32] can be developed in an employee with the proper training and mentoring programs.

Whether a person's creativity can be developed is less certain—findings in the academic literature are mixed in terms of creativity development.

Thus, screening for creativity in the hiring process is probably more important than screening for a learning orientation or emotional intelligence. It is likely that you can teach your employees to be more creative, but the research is not clear in just how much someone can be taught to be creative. Evidently, if it is communicated that the creative generation of surprise ideas is important for advancement in your firm, your employees can be guided in the right direction.

It is also useful to know that sentence completion tasks can be used in the employee selection process as a means of assessing candidates' learning orientation and emotional intelligence. In a sentence completion task, you provide a job applicant a sentence stem and ask him or her to complete the stem with the first thought that comes to mind. For example, to gauge learning orientation, the following sentence stem could be provided to the candidate: "When I complete a task in which results are unclear, I _____."

The sentence completion approach has advantages over asking job candidates to respond to Likert-type scales (ranging from "strongly agree" to "strongly disagree") measuring constructs because the Likert-type approach can be hampered by social desirability bias (the job candidate predicts how the potential employer wants the items answered). On the contrary, sentence completion tasks typically circumvent problems associated with social desirability bias because the job candidates complete the sentence stems without being aware of the specific issue that is being assessed.[33,34] For the best results, multiple forms of assessments can be combined in the hiring process. All methods are straightforward and cost and time effective. For small firms, you can pick and choose methods as you see fit. Certainly, adding some interviewing questions that assess creativity, learning orientation, and emotional intelligence would have no downside—doing so would only help ensure that you are hiring the best possible candidate—one that is most likely to derive and implement customer surprise ideas.

To summarize this chapter, fostering a culture in which a steady stream of innovative customer surprise ideas is generated requires that employees be creative. Therefore, you should attempt to attract a creative applicant pool and screen for creativity in your selection process. Even if someone is creative, she or he will likely not contribute the creative energy and talent to firm innovation unless she or he has a high level of emotional intelligence and a learning orientation. Consequently, both of these items should also be assessed in the hiring process. The end goal is a person who will have the ability and motivation to surprise customers with innovative surprise ideas.

Sure, it is easy to sit in an "ivory tower" and explain to others what would be ideal in their business ventures. Often, however, situations are not ideal. So, which of the concepts discussed in this chapter are most critical in shaping an employee's behaviors? A 2014 study examining employees' "boundary spanning creativity" in service firms found the largest determinants of employees' creativity to be: their knowledge, their emotional intelligence, and the level of managerial feedback afforded to them.[35]

Key Takeaways

- An employee's ability to surprise depends on his or her levels of creativity, learning orientation, and emotional intelligence.
- A firm's image and job postings should be designed to attract job applicants that possess creative abilities.
- Job applicants' levels of creativity, learning orientation, and emotional intelligence can be assessed in the selection process.
- Employees' levels of emotional intelligence and learning orientation can be further developed once hired.

CHAPTER 8

Expertise Awareness in Organizational Relationships

Introduction

The best customer surprise strategies are often the result of employees within a firm collaborating in idea generation and implementation. Such collaboration is significantly enhanced if employees know where one another's expertise lies. Therefore, this chapter details ways to increase expertise awareness between employees.

a·ware·ness / uh-wair-nis/ noun

1. the state or condition of being aware; having knowledge
2. consciousness

In his recent book, *Uplifting Service*, well-known customer service author Ron Kaufman suggests the following item when interviewing job candidates as a means to gain insights into their service mentalities: "Tell me how you achieved one of your greatest service successes."[1] Responses to this item should have more "us," "our," and "we" than "I," "my," and "me." Simply stated, the greatest service successes often mandate a team effort. The same holds true for deriving and implementing surprise ideas: team efforts often produce the best creativity and success.

Group creativity within your firm is not simply the sum of all of your employees' creativity efforts. Innovation and creativity within your organization is, in part, a social process. That is, the creative output of your firm depends largely on the natural interactions between individuals. Former chairman and CEO of Citibank and Citicorp addressed this topic by saying: "The person who figures out how to harness the collective genius of his or her organization is going to blow the competition away." In other words, the combined or multiplicative efforts of a team can far exceed the sum of the individual efforts. Yes, one of your employees might derive a unique surprise idea and another one of your employees might derive another very good surprise idea, but if they combine their expertise and brainstorm for ideas together the result can often far exceed the individual efforts.

Consider two technology-related surprise scenarios in the service sector. First is the utilization of technology at the gas pump that enables customers to place food orders at the pump while their gas tanks are filling. This was a game-changer in the gas and convenience store business that triggered positive surprises for many. Second, Disney World in Orlando is testing a new smart band bracelet termed *The Magic Band* that can potentially serve as a guest's room key and theme park ticket. If implemented, visitors will also have the capability to interface with the FastPass+ system and pay for within-park purchases.[2]

Technology properly advanced is indistinguishable from magic.
—Arthur C. Clarke

In both of these cases, a single individual did not possess the expertise to bring these ideas to the game floor. The best customer surprise tactics are often developed and implemented through team efforts.

How would the employees know to work together to generate novel surprise ideas? With regard to group dynamics, we will begin by considering the issue of expertise awareness. Why would you ever think to approach *colleague B* for help on a project if you did not know that *colleague B* possesses expertise that could be useful to the project?

Evidently, each person within an organization possesses a unique set of experiences and a unique set of talents that can be utilized to derive creative customer delight tactics. Therefore, the most innovative firms create cross-functional and cross-departmental teams so that individuals in typically disparate areas can become aware of each others' expertise. Each Ritz–Carlton hotel, for example, has what is termed a T-3 team composed of a cross-section of team members.[3] These teams serve a number of roles, but most pertain to deriving ways to deliver top-rate and memorable guest experiences.

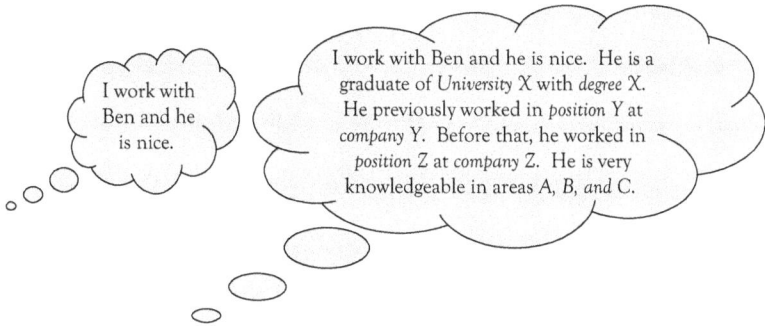

To recap these discussions, the act of soliciting information from someone in a given situation hinges upon one's awareness of another person's expertise[4] For nearly 3 decades, researchers have documented that communication within organizations can significantly enhance creativity within those organizations.[5,6] Hence, information such as work experience, training, educational qualifications, and other work-related experience should be disseminated when pertinent to knowledge-exchange opportunities, which could aid innovation. If a particular manager possesses extensive knowledge regarding the analysis of consumers' blog postings then that expertise must be communicated. Likewise, if a particular manager has expertise in designing customer surveys, then this information should also be shared.

The practice of 360 degree interviewing can aid in this effort to disseminate information about one's expertise areas. In 360 degree interviewing, a managerial or supervisory-level job candidate is interviewed by potential supervisors, coworkers, and subordinates. Permitting associates to interview their perspective manager engenders a sense of empowerment and buy-in, but is also useful in spreading information about the candidate's experience and track-record across multiple levels of the organization. When a candidate is then selected, a number of individuals are already aware of the new hire's expertise areas and the new hire has already conversed with individuals at several layers in the organization.

Other tactics to spawn expertise awareness can be integrated into your company's social events. For example, tidbits of information regarding individuals' backgrounds can be randomly distributed and contests during the social event could include matching the background information with the appropriate individual. Measures such as this can not only

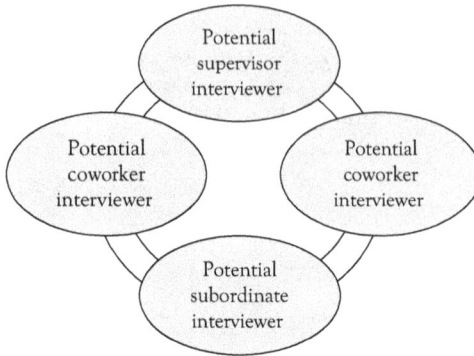

build cohesiveness, but also aid expertise awareness. Plus, such games are fun when prizes are involved.

Workspace design can also have a significant influence on information awareness and resulting collaboration. I remember back to when I was a chef at a large hotel many years ago. There were three offices along a particular corridor: the chefs occupied one and the restaurant managers occupied the other two. After a couple of months of lackluster comment card ratings deriving from the restaurant to which I was assigned, one of the hotel's executives made the decision to shuffle office space in an attempt to address the stagnant performance. He detected (accurately so) communication barriers between the chefs and the restaurant managers and his solution to rectify this problem was to make us share office space. Looking back nearly 20 years later I am still surprised at the degree to which workspace design can impact collaboration. Sharing offices improved communication and collaboration exponentially over the previous setup, which placed us down the hall—and the hallway was short—only 20 to 30 feet long. When the offices were shared, our conversations could not end with simple greetings, pleasantries, and comments about the weather. Being in the same office, our conversations naturally extended in frequency and depth. What was the common conversation point?—the restaurant, of course. We learned each other's backgrounds and tendencies much better, and improved performance was a consequence.

The notion of configuring office space to maximize collaboration is a concept that began gaining attention in the 1980s. Hewlett-Packard would physically group the engineer, the marketer, and the manufacturer together at the inception of a project. Similar stories can be told of 3M.[7]

It is prudent to note that in some service businesses the opportunity for collaboration exists in vehicles (literally vehicles: e.g., cars and trucks) as your employees move from one service location to the next. If your business model entails transporting employees between service delivery locations, you will notice that particular employees will tend to ride and sit together. Just as with office space assignments, you should consider intervening to shuffle such patterns to improve collaboration.

There is actually a sizable body of research about how workspace configuration and characteristics can influence collaboration. A number of studies demonstrate how physical space traits and configurations can either enhance or impede collaboration. Upon sifting through significant portions of this research, I have concluded that it is unwise to make general statements about how spaces should or should not be set up. Your firm is a living entity and the health of its configuration and layout is context specific. For some firms, workplace ping pong and foosball tables would enhance collaboration, whereas in other firms such amenities would be distracting, and in other firms they would be awkward and unutilized. In summary, there is no magic-bullet, no one-size-fits-all solution. Just know that the appropriate workspace environment can significantly enhance information awareness between your team members.

There are recent reports that some firms have gone so far as to take away dedicated office space assignments in an effort to increase collaboration. Each employee is issued a locker that contains a power outlet so that she or he can charge laptops and mobile devices. Beyond the locker assignment, no other spaces have permanent obligations. Workers simply reserve a physical space (via their mobile devices) depending on what tasks they need to accomplish in the given day. Thus, there are spaces that can be reserved that are conducive for team collaboration (round tables) and well as spaces that can be reserved for silent work (long rows of workstations). If a worker feels like doing some exercise, a walking desk (a desktop on a treadmill) can be reserved.

Other than adjustments to the physical space, what further measures can be put in place to enhance expertise exchange in your workplace? Team-based contests designed in the workplace that reward the delivery of customer surprises can prove useful. A research experiment published in 2013 conducted by Hua Chen, a business professor at the University of Mississippi, and Noah Lim, a business professor at the University of Wisconsin-Madison, found that team-based contests are more motivating than individual-based contests when participants know each other (such as in a work setting). This motivation toward high performance is driven by not wanting to let the team down.[8]

The final point in this chapter is that you should create as many bridge builders as possible. That is, all organizations have social networks that can be described as subsets of established informal relations that exist across units or departments.[9] Bridge builders are people who actively work to send these social networks across new nodes and branches. In simple terms, bridge building entails linking people who are not already connected.

Because of your passion for your organization, whether you realize it or not, you are likely already a bridge builder. That is, you probably already work to connect people within your firm whose collaboration could improve the customer experience. The key, however, is to motivate others to be bridge builders as well. Certainly, all managers in your firm should be active bridge builders. Department or unit-based silos are not healthy for the firm and do not bring value to the customer experience. How can the best customer surprise ideas be generated and effectively implemented if diverse sets of expertise are not cross-pollinated for the benefit of the firm?

Key Takeaways

- Often employees' combined efforts in creating and implementing customer surprise tactics have the potential to exceed their individual efforts.
- Employees should be aware of where one another's expertise lies so that they can collaborate efficiently.
- 360 degree interviewing, various social activities, work space design, and team-based contests have each been shown to influence expertise awareness among employees.
- Bridge builders who possess the ability to foster meaningful connections between individuals are valuable to organizations.

CHAPTER 9

Expertise Access in Organizational Relationships

Introduction

As detailed in the previous chapter, the best customer surprise strategies are often the result of employees working together in idea generation and implementation. Therefore, this chapter outlines the means by which employees can feel that they have access to one another's expertise.

ac·cess / ak-ses / *noun*

1. the ability, right, or permission to approach, enter, speak with, or use; admittance;
2. the state or quality of being approachable;
3. a way or means of approach.

Awareness is not enough. For your employees to collaborate to create surprise ideas they need to feel comfortable exchanging information.

I am currently a professor in a business school at a large university. It has been my observation that the stereotype of a professor being absent-minded, socially awkward, and reclusive is largely inaccurate (honestly). But, there are some who prefer not to come out of their shells and collaborate with individuals unfamiliar to them. Thus, *professor A* might know that *professor*

B has a particular expertise, but *professor A* might feel uncomfortable approaching him or her. In other words, she or he feels as if she or he does not have access to him or her because one or both of them are shy and reclusive. As a consequence of such reluctance, leading universities have recently derived an effective solution to resolve this innovation barrier: they created cross-disciplinary "centers" with particular themes. For example, there might be a "service innovation" center. The universities then implement strong incentives for professors to collaborate within the centers. In many cases, the multidisciplinary nature of a research team is a key criterion in the research grant funding decision. For instance, while it might be possible for a team of three hospitality professors to win a grant award on a service innovation project, a multidisciplinary team comprised of individuals from disparate fields (e.g., hospitality, computer science, linguistics, and theater) would have a better likelihood of securing the award. In other words, many universities have created incentives for open collaboration that could spawn innovation. The key is a sense of access—university administrators want professors in disparate fields of study to access each other's expertise.

Therefore, access is another relationship factor that influences the generation of innovative ideas capable of surprising customers. To recap the prior discussions, *manager A* might be aware that *manager B* possesses a particular expertise, but may also feel that she or he does not have access to *manager B*.[1,2] In business, no decisions are made with all the possible information, but rather decision makers satisfice when they feel that they have enough information. This point of satisfice is a function of the ease with which information is located. Thus, if the managers within your firm do not feel that they can easily access each others' expertise, then this lack of access hinders innovation.

In the age of cell phones and text-messaging, if *manager A* does not feel that she or he has access to *manager B's* knowledge, the problem rarely lies in the inability of the two to make contact, but rather in the comfort level of the relationship between the individuals. It, therefore, becomes your responsibility to foster an organizational climate that reduces such access barriers.

When Henry Kissinger was the U.S. secretary of state he asked a young Rhode Scholar to write a report on a particular topic. The young man took about 2 weeks to craft the report, and, 2 days after submitting it to Kissinger, it was returned to him with a note that read: "This is awful, do it again."

Embarrassed, the young man revised and resubmitted it to Kissinger. In response to this iteration, Kissinger wrote: "This is worse than the first version; can't you do better?"

The young man revised the document again and attached the following note: "It may not be good enough and I'm sorry for wasting your time. But this is the best I can possibly do on this subject. I'm sorry it took so long." In response Kissinger wrote: "I'll read it now."[3]

The point to this Kissinger story is that some organizations have various forms of hazing that serve as rites of passage for those junior in the organization. If orchestrated properly, such tactics can serve as useful developmental tools for maturation in the firm. But…if orchestrated poorly, such tactics can hinder information access in the long run and harm information sharing that could have led to the generation of novel ideas. Eventually there must be a transition in which the hazing is complete and rapport between coworkers is established: strong rapport in which individuals feel as if they can access each other's expertise.

With regard to rapport, perceived norms of reciprocity influence levels of rapport: "If I ask for help or advice, what is going to be expected of me in return?" In order for the knowledge to be sought, the information seeker must assess that the information is not too costly in terms of interpersonal repercussions or obligations. An example of an interpersonal repercussion would be the risk of admitting ignorance in a given area.[4] Also, obligations can come in the form of expected reciprocity. A person may ask: "Is the debt that I owe to the information provider worth it?" Perceptions of high interpersonal debt will thwart the exchange of knowledge and encourage information hoarding, consequently hindering rapport.

When groups collaborate, information sharing is enhanced when criticism is framed as a set of questions. Criticism is sometimes needed when information is being exchanged; hence, the saying "When two people in business always agree, then one of them is not necessary." The key, however, is how tactfully the criticism is presented. I remember an instance when I was a member of an award selection committee and one of the committee members had concern regarding the validity of one of the nominee's credentials. Rather than outwardly criticizing, he instead communicated his concern through a series of questions to the committee—the strategy was quite effective. When responses were formulated to his questions, his concerns become clear to the group.

Information access between individuals not only depends on rapport, but trust as well. There are two types of trust that need to be considered here. First, process-based trust is a form of trust that relies on past and expected future exchanges between the same parties.[5] If individuals develop a track record of successful collaboration, then process-based trust is formed, and access to each other's expertise is enhanced. For example, if two coworkers have worked together successfully on several occasions to implement new ways of surprising customers, then the process-based trust between these coworkers strengthens through time as a result of these successful collaborations.

Character-based trust is a form of trust that often hinges on whether individuals have common cultural or ethnic identities.[6] Research indicates that even the most open-minded individuals are often quicker to trust someone of their own culture than someone outside their culture. In many cases, this is even a subconscious and unrealized bias. Thus, if you employ a culturally or ethnically diverse group, you must find ways to increase dialogue and resulting trust between parties. Pot luck gatherings, for instance, are often useful in achieving this end. In a pot luck gathering in which individuals are encouraged to contribute ethnic dishes, often conversations emerge, which help to reduce cultural distance and foster bonds that can help root relationships.

Regardless of ethnicity, as well as other factors, some people are simply natural collaborators. Research indicates that in some organizations a few key people drive collaboration, and, if those people were to leave, collaboration between departments would likely be reduced by more than 50 percent.[7] To spread this behavior across a wider group, success stories that stem from collaboration should be publicized within your firm. Content notifications and alerts that describe these success stories can be sent across internal communication systems encouraging more individuals to collaborate. For example, if a consumer discusses in an Internet blog posting that two of your firm's employees worked together to help solve a script-deviating problem, then this posting should be shared across internal channels.

Regarding IT systems, some are set up to encourage collaboration more so than others. For example, there are some IT systems used at car rental locations in which notes inputted at one location about customer history and preferences can be viewed at another location. This history and preference information can be used to create positive surprises. For instance, a manager at *location A* can enter into the system that a particular customer requested extra leg room. At *location B*, the customer can be pleasantly surprised by being offered a vehicle with maximum leg room. Although the notes in such an IT system make it easier to positively surprise customers, currently not all firms possess this capability in their IT systems. Customer information details, access, and sharing should be high priorities when selecting and upgrading systems.

If your business model entails multiple locations, if time and money permit, emerging research finds that site visits designed so that associates can visit one another's locations significantly aid team cohesion and performance.[8] That is, if team members can actually see where one another works and under what conditions, then they get to know each other on a different level. Such coworker familiarity fosters the team's performance including the level of creativity produced.

To carry the aforementioned logic one step further, occasional "best practice exchange" seminars can also be very useful. I recently led one of these seminars for a service company that manages approximately 40 locations. The managers of the locations were gathered for 2 days of meetings, one of which was my 90-minute "best practice exchange." It involved me introducing a topic of conversation, discussing some of the emerging research on the topic, and then asking the managers to discuss some of the best ways that they have found to handle that area. After approximately 10 to 15 minutes we would then move to the next topic. The value in this format is that managers learned new ideas from each other. We even witnessed a snowballing effect in which one response triggered a thought in someone else. In fact, many of the brainstorming categories were centered on the topic of this book. For example, we discussed positively surprising customers as well as handling failure situations in which customers have heightened attention due to their script deviations.

How important is such collaboration in deriving customer delight ideas? Researchers representing the University of Virginia and McKinsey and Company once wrote the following in the *Harvard Business Review* about within-company social networks:

> When is a company greater than the sum of its parts? When its once-siloed business units find a way to harvest innovations in the white spaces between them.[9]

In the same article, the authors wrote:

> Executives can't simply hope that collaboration will spontaneously occur in the right place at the right times in their organizations.

Rather than hoping that collaboration will spontaneously occur, your firm must have robust measures in place that foster expertise awareness and interpersonal access. These are key components in sustaining a culture in which delight tactics are systematically derived and orchestrated in your customers' experiences. If you couple these relationship-level factors with high employee satisfaction and creativity, then you are well on your way to having your delight tactics serve as one of your sustainable competitive advantages.

To further illustrate the importance of expertise sharing in deriving surprises, consider the following diagrams:

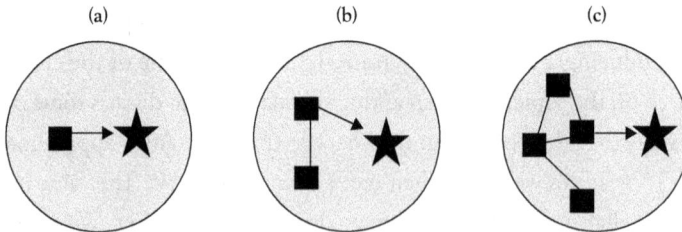

(a)   (b)   (c)

In the diagrams, the squares represent employees, the star signifies a customer, the lines denote collaboration, and the arrows represent the delivery of a surprise. Evidently, not all consumer surprises are created equal; therefore, who do you think among A, B, or C will trigger the highest degree of surprise? The answer is C for two potential reasons: (1) surprise C will be least common due to the collaboration that is needed, and (2) consumers can often sense the degree of effort that a firm has put into deriving a particular surprise tactic.

In an attempt to further emphasize the importance of team collaboration in surprise strategies, let us turn to the story of a surgeon who routinely completes knee replacement surgeries in 20 minutes. Yes, a knee replacement in 20 minutes. This rate permits him to perform more than 550 replacements per year, which is approximately two to three times the efficiency rate of many other surgeons. More importantly, his procedures have higher success rates and fewer complications than the current norms in the knee replacement industry. Interestingly, he largely attributes his accuracy and efficiency to the fact that his two teams of surgical aids have high levels of cohesiveness and have been working with him and each other for years.[10] In other words, their "team familiarity" drives their performance and their consequent ability to deliver delight to patients.

In 2013, three McKinsey and Company executives, Alex Rawson, Ewan Duncan, and Conor Jones, published an article titled "The Truth about Customer Experience" in the Harvard Business Review. This interesting and informative article made a point that zeroes-in on the importance of teamwork (p. 7): "Even if a fix appears obvious from the outside, the root causes of poor customer experience stem from the inside, often from cross-functional disconnects."[11] In other words, the quintessential role of teamwork in spawning top-rate service experiences cannot be downplayed.

Now for the next step creating a surprise culture:

> Although information sharing and cohesiveness among employees are useful in delivering top-rate customer surprises, the other side of the coin entails understanding your customers well enough to derive surprise tactics that will be salient and value adding in their experiences. We turn to this topic in the coming section.

Key Takeaways

- Employees should feel as if they have access to one another's information so that they can collaborate efficiently.

- Both rapport and trust between employees have been demonstrated to influence perceived information access among them.
- IT systems can also have a significant impact on the level of information access among employees.
- Best practice exchange seminars can be useful in bolstering information access among individuals.

PART IV

Generating Surprise Ideas: A Customer's Perspective

Preview

A genuine understanding of who your customers are, what they like and dislike, and how they perceive their surroundings, aids in generating surprise ideas. Gaining such an understanding of your customers requires that you and your team establish a rapport with them, so that they feel comfortable conversing and sharing their thoughts and perceptions with you. Similarly, there are also some less-direct means of generating surprise ideas for your firm by gaining information about your competitors and their customers. Because service ideas cannot be patented, ideas located through scanning both inside and outside of your industry can be implemented in your firm.

CHAPTER 10

Rapport Building With Your Customers

Introduction

If the service provider and the customer have a good rapport then the service provider will know better how to delight him or her. Therefore, this chapter addresses rapport building between the client and provider.

Rapport is said to exist between two people when they feel comfortable around each other and "click" with each other. Stated differently, they feel that their interaction has a good "chemistry." Rapport is important in surprise idea generation because if you and your team understand your customers well enough to know what ideas would positively surprise them, then it is much easier to implement these ideas. The rapport that you and your team build with your customers will aid in this effort because researchers identify information sharing as a defining feature of rapport.[1]

To restate, establishing a high level of rapport with your customers will help you surprise them because they will share more of their information with you. If you have rapport, then a customer might mention that it is his wife's birthday—an opportunity to surprise. With good rapport, a couple might mention that it is their wedding anniversary—an opportunity to surprise. A customer might also mention that she is nervous about an upcoming sales presentation—an opportunity to surprise. In a similar vein, if you have rapport, then a customer might mention to you that she or he just experienced a script deviation before arriving at your firm—a canceled flight, car trouble, and so forth. Due to these script deviations before your transaction, now you know that you have their full attention and you can impress. In summary, rapport significantly aids the generation of delight ideas.

Here is an example of the need for rapport: Just recently, I took my family to a local restaurant for dinner. I had met the manager on two occasions in the past—we can be considered acquaintances. The dinner at the restaurant did not meet our expectations. In our assessment, both the food and service were of poor quality. Because the manager was not present the night that we dined there, when he saw me next, he asked me how we found our experience. If I felt that I had rapport with him, I could have given him some useful feedback for improving the operation. Because I did not have rapport with him, I was uncertain how he would respond to frank feedback and instead gave him a very generic response. In essence, rapport can be critical to garnering useful information from your customers.

Even though
you don't feel
comfortable around
me, can you please
share your thoughts
and perceptions
with me?

The research in the area of service management and related fields provides some useful guidance on how to foster rapport between frontline service providers and customers. This chapter presents this key research.

First, rapport building can be developed in a service business if the dramaturgical metaphor is stressed at the frontline. That is, it should be stressed in your company's service training that actors (the employees), an audience (the customers), and a stage exist in the service environment. As in a theater production, the actors are on-stage when the audience can see or hear them. This dramaturgical metaphor serves as a useful metaphor that guides norms of conduct in social interactions[2] and in service environments.[3,4] Service workers who internalize this metaphor are less likely to participate in off-stage acts and conversations while on-stage than workers who do not grasp the concept. Training this concept is necessary for rapport-building because customers expect that the provider plays a certain part in the exchange and feels uncomfortable when the provider exhibits off-stage behaviors or conversations.

Witnessing on-stage behavior makes a customer feel important and valued. When she or he feels valued, she or he is more likely to return, and eventual loyalty leads to rapport. Taking all aspects of what goes into an on-stage performance, how well a provider performs contributes to the customer's total impression of the service experience.[5] The combination of utilizing consistency throughout and valuing the customer using the on-stage performance component fosters a positive impression. In turn, firms that incorporate an on-stage or off-stage component in their service training to their frontline associates will achieve better rapport building with customers than firms that do not have an on-stage or off-stage training component.

While on-stage, the service interaction is assessed, in part, based on the quality of the verbal dialogue that characterizes the exchange. Particular language and phrases serve to establish rapport.[6] Therefore, verbal coaching should be incorporated into your service training system in order to enhance rapport-building at the frontline. Weak verbal communication habits should be identified and discussed—such as asking the customer "is everything OK?" because being "OK" is a low bar to set in a service environment. Likewise, responding with "no problem" when a customer says "thank you" is also weak verbal communication in a service environment. Conversely, strong verbal communication displays should also be identified and discussed—such as calling customers by their names and personalizing conversations whenever possible. As part of this verbal communication component, employees can be coached on some of the basic ways of remembering customers' faces and names.[7]

Also concerning verbal communication, rapport can be developed through empathetic listening and attentiveness.[8] In spoken communication, empathetic listening is communicated when the service provider makes statements indicating that she or he can relate to the visitor (put him or herself in the customer's shoes). Attentiveness is communicated verbally when the provider paraphrases segments of what the customer has said. Both of these skills can be taught to frontline employees. Thus, firms that incorporate a verbal techniques component in their service training to their frontline associates will achieve better rapport building with customers than firms that do not have a verbal techniques training component.

Although training pertaining to weak and strong verbal communication is quintessentially vital, it must also be recognized that most human communication transpires through nonverbal cues and gestures.[9,10] The service provider's nonverbal behaviors can have a significant influence on a customer's rapport perceptions.[11] Learning to display proper body language habits is very important in provider–customer rapport building. People have certain expectations concerning specific nonverbal behaviors. Examples of gestures that foster rapport include (*a*) more smiling and positive facial expression; (*b*) contact, including frequent and longer mutual gaze; (*c*) more gesturing; (*d*) forward body lean; (*e*) direct body orientation and more open body position;(*f*) more head nods; (*g*) closer distance or proximity; (*h*) frequent touch (used with caution); (*i*) moderate relaxation; and (*j*) less random body movement.

Nonverbal cues such as those previously listed play a significant role in rapport building.[12] Rapport is demonstrated through mutual attentiveness. Three nonverbal indicators of attentiveness include: eye contact, physical proximity, and head nodding.[13] Furthermore, smiling is perhaps one of the most significant nonverbal rapport builders.[14] Well-known writer Dale Carnegie states it best: "Actions speak louder than words, and a smile says, 'I like you. You make me happy. I am glad to see you.'"[15] Firms that incorporate a nonverbal techniques component in their service training to their frontline associates will achieve better rapport building with customers than firms that do not have a nonverbal techniques training component.

Next, an effective rapport-building training program should teach empowerment. For example, the training should stress that in the event of a service failure, the contact employee is fully empowered to make redress decisions. Such failure recovery empowerment increases the speed of the recovery process and increases the likelihood that the contact employee will follow-through and take ownership of the situation.[16] Furthermore, empowerment increases the odds that the employee will go the extra mile for the customer because empowerment is correlated with job satisfaction.[17,18] In fact, empowerment often has more of an influence on the job satisfaction of customer contact employees than on noncontact employees.[19] Empowerment is particularly vital to the rapport-building process because if the provider is able to make decisions, then the customer can better relate to and bond with the provider because they are both actively shaping the exchange.

Rapport can also be augmented by personalizing conversations. As a result, customer rapport-building training should emphasize the skills necessary to provide personalization whenever possible. Such skills entail being attentive to the customer's verbal and nonverbal cues. Personalizing conversations begins with listening; therefore, empathetic listening skills are needed in which customers are encouraged to fully communicate their thoughts and feelings.[20] Not only should it be stressed in training that personalized service can be delivered by paying attention to the customer (both verbal and nonverbal cues), but personalized service can also be achieved in situations in which experienced workers share customer preference information with novice workers. This information exchange among service workers should be encouraged so long as it pertains to the delivery of customized interactions. Firms that incorporate a personalized attention component in their service training to their frontline associates will achieve better rapport building with visitors than firms that do not have a personalized attention training component. As customers begin to notice a firm's adaptation to their cues, the rapport between the frontline associates and customers is enhanced.

Also in terms of personalizing conversations, it is my position that all service firms should list their employees' hometowns on their name tags. Although some service firms have been doing this for decades, many still do not. The hometown information creates a conversation piece when a customer has lived in (or has family in) the same area. I remember, for instance, working in Kansas and displaying Virginia Beach, Virginia, on my name tag spawned a steady stream of conversations with customers who were prior military and had been

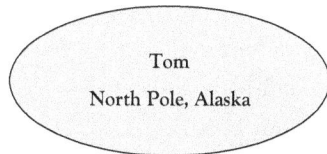

Tom
North Pole, Alaska

stationed in the Virginia Beach area in their younger years. At that hotel, my coworker displayed North Pole, Alaska, as his hometown, which also triggered regular conversations with guests simply due to the unique nature. It is not every day that we meet someone from the North Pole— and no, he did not personally know Santa Claus (a question asked by many kids staying at the hotel). Such conversations can be the building blocks in establishing rapport.

Due to the nature of interacting in real-time, it is also germane to note that stress levels can sometimes be very high in service environments.[21] Due to this stress, rapport-building training should include a composure component. Research indicates that such composure, also termed *emotional regulation*, is a trainable skill.[22,23] Developing employees' emotional intelligence, for example, aids emotional regulation.[24,25] In addition, frontline providers well educated in the flows and paths of service in their respective areas of the servicescape and the proper pacing of these *flows* can also aid with composure and emotional regulation. Composure is important for rapport building because customers want to be *assured* that providers are capable of performing their roles well. In other words, they want to be confident in the employees' abilities.

Rapport-building training should also emphasize the notion that the happier the customer the less strain she or he places on the frontline worker. Researchers term this logic the satisfaction mirror and it contends that customer satisfaction and employee satisfaction have a positive, reciprocating relationship in service firms.[26] Based on this logic, it should be emphasized to frontline employees that the better they establish rapport with the customer, the happier the customer will be in their roles. Accenting this concept in training will serve to motivate the frontline provider to work to establish rapport with customers. Hence, firms that incorporate a satisfaction mirror component in their service training to their frontline associates will achieve better rapport building with visitors than firms that do not have a satisfaction mirror training component.

Just because you offer rapport-building training to your employees does not necessarily mean that the training will be effective in influencing their customer-contact behaviors. Select studies have found that there is not much difference in the level of performance between those who receive training and those who did not.[27,28] One study, in particular, found that 40 percent of trainees do not incorporate trained skills immediately after training; 70 percent failed to do so 1 year after training; and, ultimately, only 50 percent of training investments yield organizational improvements.[29] Can these findings be accurate? Is it possible that employee training might not be the optimum use of a firm's resources?

As detailed in my previous book, *Performance Enhancer: Twenty Essential Habits for Service Businesses*, offering training is not necessarily sufficient for influencing employees' rapport-building behaviors. Training transfer describes the degree to which trained skills actually get applied on the job.[30] For training transfer to occur, "learned behavior must be generalized to the job context and maintained over a period of time on the job."[31] One variable found to be highly correlated with transfer is the content relevance of the training materials.[32,33] Thus, the more that the firm can convince the trainee that the training is relevant to his or her job, the more training transfer will transpire. It should be stressed to the trainee that rapport that is established by applying the trained concepts in customer interactions will make his or her roles less stressful and more enjoyable.

Training transfer is highly contingent on the trainee's peer support in implementing the trained skills.[34] In your firm, if some of your employees apply the trained rapport-building skills while other reject the content, this could create a peer-pressure environment that hinders training transfer. In such a circumstance, training transfer is restricted for two reasons: (1) frontline providers deduce that if not all coworkers display the trained skills, then the skills must not be important, and (2) even if a given employee knows that the skills are important, peer-pressure might restrict displays of the trained behaviors.

Training transfer is more likely to occur if the trainee senses that his or her supervisor is genuinely committed to the rapport-building content being taught.[35,36] If you continuously signal to employees that you are committed to the given training content then you will have a better likelihood of transfer. These signals can come in many forms, but the key is to signal that you are committed to rapport-building. Of course, like any form of training, your genuine support is communicated less through what you say and more through what you do. How are your rapport building skills?

What if you operate a small firm and you do not offer service training to your employees? Well then start! Let me repeat: What if you're a small firm and you don't offer service training to your employees? Well then start! All of the items in this chapter can be incorporated into your daily shift huddles. You could cover one item per day. You do not need to dedicate the entire shift huddle to the topic; instead, it can be piggybacked on whatever other information needs to be covered on a given day. After you have covered all of the topics, it is recommended that you rotate back through them every few months. All learners—including adults—learn best through repetition.

To conclude this chapter, rapport with your customers significantly aids your ability to generate surprise ideas. Such rapport is particularly necessary when deriving ideas to surprise your regular customers. A group of researchers once described rapport as the "quality of [a] relationship characterized by satisfactory communication and mutual understanding."[37] Such mutual understanding cultivates a dialogue with your customers so that you can enhance your understanding of their expectations, wants, and perceptions.

We end with the following analogy: Is it easier to pick out the "perfect" birthday present for a stranger or for someone who you know well? The answer is obvious. This logic extends to offering surprise ideas: If you know someone well it is easier to find creative ways to make them happy. To get to know someone well, you must first establish rapport.

Key Takeaways

- Successfully formulating and carrying out customer surprise ideas is positively correlated with the level of rapport between the provider and customer.
- Training frontline employees in the drama metaphor as well as empathetic listening skills, aids rapport building.
- Training frontline employees in strong verbal communication skills bolsters rapport building.
- Empowering frontline employees with decision-making authority aids rapport building.
- Employee training is most effective when measures are in place to ensure training transfer.

CHAPTER 11

Feedback From Your Customers

Introduction

This chapter discusses means by which to gather customer feedback, which can be used by the firm to better understand how to orchestrate surprise strategies.

If you establish rapport with your customers, they will be eager to share key information with you. The next step, therefore, is to provide avenues that make it easy for them to share this information. Also, you will need to be a good listener.

For a number of years I have been analyzing the customer satisfaction surveys collected by an outdoor recreation provider with several dozen locations. If this recreation provider were a publicly traded company, I would load up on their stock. Every indicator signals to me that they are a healthy organization: Satisfaction scores on the surveys are near perfect every year, repurchase intent reported on the surveys hovers around 98 percent each year, word-of-mouth intent about the same, and, every year at the management meeting, I see the same faces—very low turnover.

Here is the catch: In the "comments" section of the survey about one out of six surveys details a hand-written complaint from a patron. How can approximately one out of six survey respondents complain and the satisfaction scores, repurchase, and word-of-mouth scores be exceptionally high year in and year out? Well, when I am analyzing the surveys, I cannot distinguish between complaints and suggestions for improvement—they are one and the same. For instance, if someone writes that the hours for the boat rental facility should be extended—is this a complaint or a suggestion for improvement? The fact of the matter is that every year, there are about 180,000 words of this written feedback provided by their customers.

The bottom line is that the patrons like the establishments so well and feel such a strong connection and rapport with them that they feel comfortable providing this sort of feedback. The provider then uses this feedback to improve the offerings. It is a cycle: first-rate offerings ➔ satisfaction and loyalty ➔ rapport ➔ feedback ➔ refinement of offerings. This example from the recreation sector is used to illustrate the power of rapport and the importance of making your customers feel comfortable in providing you with feedback.

Research has long demonstrated that open channels of communication are critical to monitoring customer satisfaction, but are also important for detecting emerging problems and anticipating changes by discovering customer–service interactions that deviate from scripts and genuinely improve the interaction experience.[1] A customer orientation that empowers a more involved customer yields a more binding and satisfying relationship. The relationship is not one way, but give-and-take, so that long-standing service processes can be refined and innovative surprise ideas can be introduced.[2]

Within the context of customer surprise, what is the most pressing information to elicit from your customers? Hofstra University professor, Dr. Barry Berman, has conducted research and written on the subject of customer delight for a number of years. One article, in particular, published in the *California Management Review*, contains a list of questions that a firm should ask itself to help in determining if optimal delight programs are in place.[3] The questions are, in essence, an internal audit. Listed in the following figure are adaptations of some of the questions that are most germane to the context of this book.

How do you extract the answers to these questions from your customers? In Tom Connellan's book, *Inside the Magic Kingdom*, he makes a statement with which I heartily agree: "Customers are best heard through many ears."[4] In the book he describes how Disney uses multiple approaches to gathering and analyzing customer information. Each means

Does your firm…

…identify the domains where customers have expectations?

…identify the domains where customers do not have expectations?

…study how customer expectation sets differ among its major market segments?

…determine how customer expectation sets change over time?

…understand the difficulties of continually delighting customers?

…evaluate alternative customer delight delivery strategies?

…examine how other companies delight customers?

…continuously monitor customer delight levels?

of gathering and analyzing customer information has strengths and weaknesses. Multiple techniques should be used by all firms.

First, customer conversations are critical. Your customers would be glad to engage in meaningful conversations with you and your team members once rapport-laden relationships are established. In his book *Keeping Clients Satisfied*, customer service author Robert Bly states the following:

> A more powerful way of assessing the client's requirements is through conversation….Effective client communication starts with the realization that communication is not a separate activity from rendering a service: Communication is a component of how you render service.[5]

Sometimes more can be learned from talking with your five best customers than through surveying 5,000 of them. Conversations with customers can be rich and meaningful. As discussed in the previous chapter, the key to having meaningful conversations with your customers is the establishment of rapport. If your customers feel comfortable describing their expectations, perceptions, and experiences with you in an open and frank dialogue, then a lot of insight can be gained. Conversations are particularly useful due to the opportunity to probe and discuss various points.

In addition to conversations, what other channels are available for such communication from your customers? As described at the beginning of this chapter, customer surveys can be a useful forum. In my assessment, most of the customer surveys that I see coming from service firms need improvement. Crafting a survey that has the potential to provide valid and useful results requires expertise. If no one in your firm has a high level of expertise or experience in designing surveys it is necessary to consult with an expert for guidance. There are a whole host of both intentional and unintentional response biases that can come into play if a poorly designed survey is put into use. Results, for example, depend on question wording and question sequencing.

Moreover, even the surveys that appear to avoid many of the common wording and sequencing pitfalls do not provide adequate insight into the questions listed earlier in this chapter. For instance, I have never seen a service firm use sentence completion tasks on a customer survey. The following sentence stems could provide a firm with rich guidance on how to design their offerings. Consider asking your customers to complete the following sentences with the first thought that comes to mind (for this illustration, let us assume that your company's name is XYZ).

- When doing business with XYZ, the thing that surprised me the most was _____

  _____ .

- XYZ is the place to go when _____

  _____ .

- If XYZ wants to make its offerings better it should

  _____ .

- If XYZ did not exist, I would have gone to

  _____ instead.

While surveys should be one tool in your consumer research arsenal, they cannot be your only tool because response rates are often very low. Most of the individuals who respond to the surveys are either extremely happy or extremely upset. In many service sectors, far more consumers detail their experiences with the firm on Internet blog posts. Why would a consumer be reluctant to complete a 3- to 4-minute survey, but then invest the effort to post a narrative on the Internet about their experience? The Internet is often the communication channel of choice because the consumer wants his or her voice heard by other consumers.

Consumers' blog postings can be golden for you. This rich and abundant information on the Internet offers many firms with opportunities to understand their customers better. The consumers' blog postings can be read, interpreted, and text-mined by your firm. Text-mining blogs can shed light on the following: What facets of the experience are consumers commenting most frequently about? What facets are they most emotional about? What surprised them? What disappointed them? What are their suggestions for improvement? What are their recommendations to other consumers? Which of your employees are doing the best job surprising your customers (as described in the blog postings)?

Do not underestimate the power of consumer blogs. I recently attended an awards ceremony for employees recognized for their customer service skills. The company went all out for the ceremony—multiple food courses including steak and shrimp—abundant decorations—music—presence of all key company executives.

To be eligible for an award, an employee had to be nominated by a manager. Of the three finalists for the most prestigious companywide award, the managers' nomination letters had one thing in common: For all three, the nomination letters largely used consumer blog postings as evidence to demonstrate the employees' customer service achievements. For example, a blog posting described how an employee went and purchased cold medication for a customer. At that awards ceremony, it was interesting that all three nominating managers turned to consumers' blog postings to gather evidence of their employees' achievements—blogs can be powerful. They provide a direct look at what the customers view as salient.

Should small firms implement the practices discussed in this chapter? It is strongly recommended that *all* firms engage in conversations and in surveying. The key is that the conversations must be meaningful, and the surveys crafted properly. Not all firms have consumer blogs available for analysis—blogging has not yet permeated all service sectors—in the future, blog analysis will be a standard practice in all sectors.

Key Takeaways

- Gathering customer feedback helps firms understand how to orchestrate surprise strategies.
- A multimethod approach should be used in gathering customer feedback.
- While surveying is a key method of gathering customer feedback, a large portion of current surveys are poorly designed: garbage-in ➜ garbage-out.
- In conjunction with surveying, qualitative methods, such as customer interviews, are also useful in better understanding their perceptions.
- In some service industries, text-mining consumer blogs can prove very useful in furthering a firm's understanding of customers' perceptions.

CHAPTER 12

Scanning the Business Environment for Surprise Ideas

Introduction

This chapter details how firms should scan both inside and outside of their industries for surprise tactics that they can implement.

In the 1980s, a biologist studying primate monkey behavior in the rainforest of Panama noted that there appeared to be a dearth of snakes in the forest. She had seen lots of monkeys, but never a snake.

Thus, one day, a fellow scientist who specializes in snake behavior went into the forest with her. Within the first minute, the colleague spotted a snake. Within another minute, he saw a second snake. In a short while, he had counted 50 snakes. The primate biologist was puzzled and she asked her colleague why she hadn't ever seen them before. He replied that it was because she was looking for monkeys.[1]

Scientists have actually coined a phrase to describe the aforementioned phenomenon: One possesses a *search image* for what she or he is looking for.[2] If you have a search image for monkeys, then that is what stands out. If you have one for snakes, then they are clear as day.

If you are a photographer, then photo opportunities jump out at you. If you are a guitarist, you are more aware of guitar sounds in music.

After implementing the ideas put forth in this book, your search image should be consumer surprise. If you see an idea at a retail store, amusement park, sporting event, or even a gas station that positively surprises you or a fellow consumer, it is yours for the taking. As previously stated, service ideas cannot be patented.

Even if you see or experience a surprise tactic that is not directly applicable to your business, you should write the idea down anyway. Keep a written log of all surprise tactics. In the written log, you should go so far as to include the surprises that you read about in newspapers, books, or on websites. Maybe someday you will marry an idea with another idea and make it suitable for delivery in your firm. Remember, creative people possess the capability of conceptually merging information from disparate sources. Even if you never apply a particular idea to your business, having written lists of creative surprise ideas is very useful in employee training.

You can locate consumer surprise ideas both inside and outside of your industry. First, let us discuss finding ideas inside your industry.

The obvious first step is for you or members of your team to regularly serve as customers at your competitors' locations so that you can witness what tactics they are utilizing. What do you want to copy? What do you not want to copy? Which tactics can be modified to fit well into your concept? Any first-hand information that you can gather might prove useful in enhancing your customers' experiences.

You can also learn quite a bit about your competitors by reading their customers' Internet blog postings. Very useful competitive intelligence from within your industry can be gathered by reading and analyzing these blog postings. Not only what consumers are saying about you, but just as importantly, what they are saying about your competitors. What things are your competitors doing that surprise customers? In fact, there are commercially available cloud-based computer programs that can be purchased which will text-mine not only consumer blogs posted about your firm, but also about your competitors. This text mining can detect nonobvious and managerially useful trends in the postings. Furthermore, these cloud-based programs can filter-out deceptive blogs (negative postings by competitors and positive postings by owners) with reasonable accuracy.

An often overlooked source of competitive intelligence in your industry is your set of vendors. Many of the vendors likely not only supply and service you, but your competitors as well. Once you establish rapport with your vendors, you can strike up casual conversations that might help you get some insights into your competition. Nothing earth-shattering such as top secret trade secrets, but "Hey, did you hear that Gary down at *firm x* is running *promotion y* next month?" Or, "Wow, I can't believe how much of *item x* Gary has been ordering lately; he's been giving them away for free to customers every Tuesday."

Also with regard to locating innovative ideas from within your industry, tradeshows and other sector-specific learning events can be helpful. Many of the ideas floating around tradeshows have never been released to consumers; thus, the surprise potential is significant. You will need to be more skilled than your competitors at understanding which of the new products have the potential for the greatest surprise return on investment.

Surprise ideas can derive from a variety of industry sources. For example, if you compete in the restaurant business, you should be glued to Guy Fieri's Food Network show *Diners, Drive-Ins and Dives*. If you work as a home contractor or landscaper, you should find many of the shows on HGTV helpful in innovating your customers' experiences. When I worked in the hotel business, I found Samantha Brown's Travel Channel show *Great Hotels* quite useful in offering novel ideas, which could be implemented in the properties where I worked. Many ideas used elsewhere in your industry have probably never been seen by your customers and offer an opportunity to surprise.

Now let us discuss locating surprise ideas from outside your industry. Often ideas from outside of your industry can be the most surprising for your customers. Consider the following examples:

- Years ago, Nike began selling their Air Jordan brand basketball shoes in briefcases. If a business person can carry a briefcase to the office, why can't a basketball player carry a briefcase to the locker room? Despite the perpetual smells of medicated ointments and itch-relief foot-powders, serious business takes place in locker rooms—strategizing precise strategies for victory. Thus, a briefcase is more than appropriate for this sort of business. With such innovation, it comes as no surprise that Nike is currently on the 28th rendition of the shoe and that the company brought in approximately $24 billion in revenue in 2012.
- The English founders of Lush, a handmade cosmetics retailer, have transplanted many innovative ideas from outside their

industry. Entering a Lush location is unmistakably similar to
entering a pastry shop. Soaps shaped as pastries, cakes, and
pies are displayed as if they are edible. People enter a pastry
shop with the intent to buy and often purchase multiple items
based on impulse. Therefore, by making the cosmetic store
look like a pastry shop, the same psychology applies—impulse
buying becomes the norm. With such creativity, it comes as
no surprise that Lush products are now sold in 830 stores in
51 countries.

- McDonald's Ray Kroc realized that department store managers had used mirrors to create illusions in their stores for
  decades; he, therefore, wondered why mirrors could not be
  used to create illusions in fast food retail space. Consequently,
  he placed a mirror (angled down slightly) behind the French
  fry holding bin in every McDonald's location so that customers can view the cooked fries as they wait in line to place their
  food orders. As a result, this visual image stimulated much
  greater sales of the product.

- A lot can be learned from the stand-up comedy industry.
  As we all know, laughter is said to be the shortest distance
  between two people. Humor is an instant stress reducer[3]
  that can very easily trigger a surprise in service settings if the
  humor is not expected. For example, it is my contention that
  all airline flight attendants should receive training from a
  comedy coach. Unexpected, yet tasteful jokes relayed over an
  airplane's public address system could really ease travel stress
  and trigger delight. The same holds true for physicians. When
  I go to my annual physical, I would be shocked if my doctor
  told me a joke or two—wouldn't you be surprised as well?

- Restaurants could take some notes from the casino and
  gaming industry. Imagine that when your server delivers your
  bill to your table at the end of your meal, he rolls out a large
  wheel along with it. You are granted a spin to determine the
  size of your discount: 5 percent, 10 percent, 20 percent, or
  free meal (jackpot). Not expecting this opportunity would
  leave you entertained and delighted.

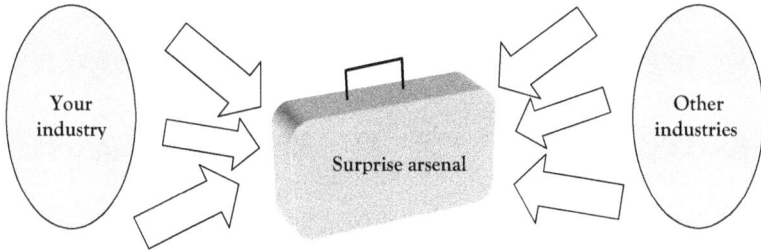

The key is your search image. Your search image should be consumer surprise ideas. Novel ideas are out there ripe for adoption in your firm. Ideas can come from inside your industry or from other sectors. Through time it actually becomes fun scanning for these creative ideas, especially when all folks on your team are scanning. Even if ideas cannot be adapted directly, they can be modified to fit your business model and customer transaction style. In his book, *The Little Big Things*, bestselling author Tom Peters suggests that all firms should mandate that each key manager be required to bring a novel idea to the table for consideration at least once per week.[4] I agree. Those in your firm should constantly scan for and bring novel surprise ideas to the table. Just as the figure suggests, you develop a *surprise arsenal* of tactics derived from both inside and outside of your industry. Your success in the service sector depends upon your surprise arsenal and both of these words are important. *Surprise* is vital in spawning script deviations to gain consumers' attention, and *arsenal* is critical in suggesting that tactics should be stored and used based on context and situation.

As you scan outside of your industry for surprise ideas you may find firms willing to help you to surprise your customers in exchange for exposure to them. Companies such as GEICO have donated funds to install iPads in airport terminals in exchange for the "sponsorship" of the terminal. Porsche has donated eight $50,000 cars to Delta airlines as a means of surprising the travelers who have tight connection times and need to get across the tarmac quickly.

Key Takeaways

- Upon reading this book, a firm's *search image* should be customer surprise tactics.

- Owners and managers should write reminder notes to themselves as they witness unique surprise tactics outside of their firms.
- Consumers' blog postings can be useful in identifying customer surprise tactics used by competitors.
- Discussions with suppliers and vendors can be useful in ascertaining customer surprise tactics used by competitors.
- The most innovative customer surprise tactics usually derive from outside of one's industry.

Final Thought

3 + 4 = 9 or 10

People will forget what you said,
People will forget what you did,
but people will never forget how
you made them feel.
— Maya Angelou

Surprise is a powerful emotion. From a physiological point of view, research indicates that surprise shares many of the same salient features as anger and fear.[1] These three emotions arouse many of the same bodily responses. From a pragmatic point of view, it would obviously be unwise to intentionally anger or scare your customers. You can, however, surprise them to win their attention.

Insurance adjusters in the housing sector are unique—they already have their customer's full attention when they show up. A tornado, derecho, hurricane, fire, mudslide, or other disaster caused the script deviation. Therefore, heightened attention begins before contact is made with the service provider. Tree care experts, roofers, medical first responders, and others may also find themselves in similar situations. A surprise has occurred, which prompted the service situation.

There are times similar cases also occur in airports when unexpected flight delays are triggered. The most innovative airports now have one or more members on staff who can quickly change into clown costumes to entertain kids with balloon animals and tricks to capitalize on the travelers' heightened attention. These circumstances, however, are rare in the service sector: In most situations, we must create the script deviation to win customer attention.

Corporate strategist and author Kenichi Ohmae once wrote: "To a person with a hammer all problems look like nails."[2] If market share falls and this is characterized by eroding customer loyalty and lack of referrals often the reflex of management is to seek to improve service delivery consistency. Although this reflex might help, it may not be what is prescribed for the situation.

Contrary to the logic contained in many business books, being consistent is not good enough in business. We can think of many service businesses that provided a consistent offering, but eventually failed despite the consistency. Today's consumers are bombarded with stimuli; thus, being consistent will not win their attention. Small surprises that cause deviations from their preformulated mental scripts will win their attention. And, will win it immediately.

"Getting the fundamentals right" is not good enough in the mature service sectors that are oversaturated with competitors. I argue that simply "getting the fundamentals right" is also not good enough in sectors that are also *currently* lacking competition because currently is the key word. In summary, all service firms should foster cultures in which a constant stream of surprise ideas are generated and demonstrated.

On a 10-point satisfaction scale (with 10 being the highest possible rating), if one of your customers responds with a 7 or 8 she or he may or may not desire to return. With such scores, she or he will not spread negative word-of-mouth, but may not be impressed enough to repurchase. In fact, a growing body of research finds that merely satisfied customers (those that provide 7s and 8s) often defect to competitors.[3, 4] Ratings of 9s and 10s, however, are different. Such ratings are directly linked to loyalty and repurchase.

Ratings of 9s and 10s on customer surveys are so important that, in recent years, in many service firms, the portion of a manager's bonus compensation designed to reward managers for excellent customer sentiment is tabulated as the percentage of customers rating the firm with 9s or 10s. In other words, in many service firms, if a customer rates an experience with the company with 7s or 8s, then the manager does not receive any monetary reward for those ratings—only 9s and 10s bring in bonus money.

How are 9s and 10s achieved? The answer resides largely in Parts 3 and 4 of this book (Hence the title of this chapter). Part 3 details the need to foster an organization-wide climate in which your employees derive a consistent stream of surprise ideas. Part 4 drives home the need to understand your customers well enough that you can surprise them with things that are meaningful enough to cause script deviations and heightened attention.

Surprises, more than simply satisfying experiences, tend to have much stronger memory traces for consumers. In other words, transactions characterized with delight are much more memorable than ones perceived as satisfactory.[5] Even as early as 1990, three leading services marketing scholars—Drs. Mary Jo Bitner, Bernard Booms, and Mary Stanfield Tetreault—published an article in the *Journal of Marketing* that detailed the results of asking consumers to recall memories of some of their best and worst service experiences.[6] The findings revealed that script deviations are what consumers really remember well: Positive and negative deviations. When unexpected things happen—your customers pay attention—this is your chance to shine.

You and your employees must continuously derive surprise ideas, even for your regular customers. Your employees' efforts will hinge upon their motivation and their ability. As stated in Chapter 7, research regarding whether an individual's creativity can be developed through training is mixed, but there is an alternative body of research that is clear: Training programs can improve the creativity of a group.[7,8] As stated previously, the creativity of a group is not the sum of the individuals' creativity. The importance of both expertise awareness and expertise access needs to be clearly communicated in organization-wide training initiatives. Training programs must communicate leadership support for the fostering of innovative surprise ideas.

Leadership support can also be communicated through the various reward programs that you design for your employees. For example, many of the large service firms have recently adopted programs in which their employees are formally recognized and rewarded for being positively mentioned by a customer on an Internet blog. In short, employee reward programs can be as varied and creative as the customer surprise tactics themselves. There are limitless ways to structure reward programs: If one of your employees does an outstanding job delighting a customer, consider sending a thank you card to his or her house. Or, hand him or her a crisp $100 bill.

Consider writing a song containing a list of ways that your employees have surprised customers and sing it at the next company party. A rap song sung by you describing how your employees go the extra mile to surprise would likely be a big hit. Doing so wouldn't be too difficult; a lot of words rhyme with surprise: highs, size, rise, lies, buys, and others. A lot of subsequent water cooler talk would be generated about your rap performance—and remember, the theme of the song was customer surprise. In other words, again, you are creating buzz about surprise.

The more creative you are in rewarding your employees, the more creative they will be in surprising customers: Firms reap what they sow. Rewards should not be big, but rather modest and frequent. A single huge annual award would create a superstar syndrome. Instead, you want everyone on-board with developing surprise innovations.

Not just reward systems, but employees can also be surprised with other company systems as well. For instance, posting work schedules on the company's intranet might pleasantly surprise employees because they can access the information from remote locations with their mobile devices. Training can also be innovative and motivating. Simply offering a particular training module through a CD-ROM format does not signal that you place much value in its importance or in the development of your employees. If you pleasantly surprise your employees, they are more apt to pleasantly surprise the customers. Like with customer surprises, you must create a culture in which new employee surprises are continuously cultivated. In the 1990s, for example, a couple of business books recommended that managers should send birthday cards to their employees' homes. This was a very impactful employee motivational tool soon after the idea was derived because it was surprising—not so much anymore.

Lastly, remember that not all surprises are created equal. Research finds that surprises vary in their degree of unexpectedness.[9] Highly unique surprises have stronger memory traces than less unique ones. By definition, a surprise can be described as "the state of a person who has experienced something unexpected,"[10] but the fact of the matter is that some surprises are more *surprising* than others. Constant environmental scanning is needed to derive the best surprise ideas. If you operate a movie theater, look to restaurants for ideas. If you operate a bowling alley, look to theme parks for ideas. If you are an airline flight attendant, look to stand-up comics for ideas. If you are a salesperson, look to your minister or preacher for ideas. Options are limitless.

All surprises are also not created equal from the sense that you can surprise a customer with something that she or he somewhat values or something that she or he highly values. The key here is to understand your customers well enough to know which of your attributes and features provide them utility.

The biggest surprises with the biggest positive impacts should be told as stories around your organization. Legendary surprise stories should be told around your firm the same way that myths are told around a camp fire. Stories can be very powerful in organizations. Instead of gossiping about each other, guide your employees to gossip about how customers were wowed and surprised.

Tom Peters and Nancy Austin's classic book, *A Passion for Excellence,* discusses how one can often tell what is important to a firm by the language that is spoken within the firm.[11] You should talk of customer surprise often in your firm. Talk about surprises in your management meetings and have your employees talk about them every day in their shift huddles. You can even derive a company-specific language to term different types of surprise. A surprise early in a transaction can be called *term A* and one late in a transaction can be called *term B.* Surprising a first-time customer can be referred to with *term X* and a surprise of a longtime customer can be described by *term Y.* For that matter, why does a meeting room need to be called a "meeting room?" A term such as "innovation space" might help foster the culture that you are seeking to create. Having those within your organization speak a unique surprise language is a creative way to communicate the importance of script deviations.

Have fun surprising your customers and establishing a surprise culture in your firm. Doing so can easily become one of the most enjoyable and intrinsically rewarding aspects of your career. You will find a healthy ratio between effort and reward when surprising your customers: A ratio worth your while. To illustrate this point, the next time that you see one of your customers holding a baby, stop for a moment and play peek-a-boo with the baby. The joy that you see in their eyes (the baby and the parent) will demonstrate the intrinsically rewarding nature of delivering simple surprises.

I really don't care whether or not you succeed; you've already bought my book and your success really does not matter to me (just kidding—but surprising you likely won your attention).

In all sincerity: Good luck!

About the Author

Vincent P. Magnini, PhD is an internationally sought-after speaker, business consultant, and educator. He is a tenured faculty member in Virginia Tech's Pamplin College of Business and currently ranked as one of the top 12 most prolific hospitality researchers worldwide. Vince holds editorial board appointments on 10 of the leading research journals in his field and is a U.S. Fulbright Scholar.

Vince's most recent book, *Performance Enhancers: Twenty Essential Habits for Service Businesses,* appeared on the top 1 percent of Amazon. com's best seller ranking during January, April, and May 2014. He has been featured twice on National Public Radio's (NPR's) *With Good Reason, All Things Considered,* and has been in the *New York Times.*

Vince is the principal of the Magnini Group, a consulting practice that specializes in applying the latest marketing research to enhance the performance of service firms.

Other books by Vincent Magnini

Performance Enhancers: Twenty Essential Habits for Service Businesses

Tourist Customer Satisfaction: An Encounter Approach
(with Francis Noe and Muzaffer Uysal)

Notes

Chapter 1

1. Bawden (2001).
2. Bawden (2001).
3. Bawden (2001).
4. Roizen and Oz (2005).
5. Oulasvirta (2005).
6. Gonzalez and Mark (2004).
7. Rumbo (2002).
8. Bawden and Robinson (2009).
9. Bateson (2002).
10. Bitner, Booms, and Mohr (1994).
11. Smith and Houston (1985).
12. Axelrod (1973).
13. Zeithaml, Bitner, and Gremler (2006).
14. Axelrod (1973).
15. Kahneman (2011).
16. Stroop (1935).

Chapter 2

1. Crotts and Magnini (2011).
2. Berman (2005a).
3. Berman (2005b).
4. Oliver (1980).
5. Berman (2005b).
6. "Delight Moves Customer Responses to Next Level" (2003).
7. Reisenzein (2000a).
8. Meyer (1997).
9. Reisenzein (2000b).
10. Hart, Heskett, and Sasser (1990).
11. Magnini, Ford, Markowski, and Honeycutt (2007a).
12. Magnini, Ford, Markowski, and Honeycutt (2007b).
13. Bitner, Booms, and Tetreault (1990).
14. The Economist (n.d.).

Chapter 3

1. Magnini, Crotts, and Zehrer (2011).
2. Nunes and Dreze (2006).

Chapter 4

1. Gronroos and Voima (2013).
2. Ramdas, Teisberg, and Tucker (2012).
3. Sanborn (2004).

Chapter 5

1. Tisch and Weber (2007).
2. Kim and Mattila (2013).
3. Wernerfelt (1984).
4. Peteraf (1993).
5. Pine and Gilmore (1998).

Chapter 6

1. Enchanted Learning (n.d.).
2. Donnelly (1992).
3. Amabile (1990).
4. Barron and Harrington (1981).
5. Pascoe, Ali, and Warne (2002).
6. de Vries, van den Hoof, and Ridder (2006).
7. Cabrera, Collins, and Salgado (2006).
8. Sanborn (2004).
9. Danziger, Levav, and Avnaim-Pesso (2011).
10. Palmer, Beggs, and McMullan (2000).
11. Lind, Kanfer, and Early (1988).
12. Bies and Moag (1986).
13. Blanchard and Johnson (1981).
14. Grant (2013).
15. Heskett, Sasser, and Schlesinger (1997).
16. Gounaris and Boukis (2013).

Chapter 7

1. Gladwell (2008).
2. Torrance (1999).

3. Hoevemeyer (2005).
4. Leavy (2005).
5. Oldham and Cummings (1996).
6. Simonton (2000).
7. Drazin, Glynn, and Kazanjian (1999).
8. Malakate, Andriopoulos, and Gotsi (2007).
9. Hargadon and Sutton (1997).
10. Hargadon and Sutton (2000).
11. Rothenberg (1996).
12. Hargadon (1998).
13. Cooper (1991).
14. Cropley (2000).
15. Dweck (1986).
16. Dweck (1989).
17. Dweck and Leggett (1988).
18. Button, Mathieu, and Zajac (1996).
19. VandeWalle, Brown, Cron, and Slocum (1999).
20. VandeWalle (2001).
21. VandeWalle (2001).
22. Magnini and Honeycutt (2003).
23. Button et al. (1996).
24. Kohli, Shervani, and Challagalla (1998).
25. Salovey and Mayer (1990).
26. Salovey and Mayer (1990).
27. Mayer and Salovey (1997).
28. Hewlett, Marshall, and Sherbin (2013).
29. Magnini and Honeycutt (2003).
30. Porter and Tansky (1999).
31. Bar-On (2007).
32. Lennick (2007).
33. Boddy (2007).
34. Fisher (1993).
35. Agnihotri, Rapp, and Gabler (2014).

Chapter 8

1. Kaufman (2012).
2. Ho (2013).
3. Michelli (2008).
4. Borgatti and Cross (2003).
5. Amabile (1988).
6. Perry-Smith and Shalley (2003).

7. Peters and Austin (1985).
8. Chen and Lim (2013).
9. Hansen, Mors, and Lovas (2005).

Chapter 9

1. Borgatti and Cross (2003).
2. Cabrera, Collins, and Salgado (2006).
3. Deal and Kennedy (1982).
4. Borgatti and Cross (2003).
5. Wang and Nicholas (2005).
6. Wang and Nicholas (2005).
7. Cross, Gray, Cunningham, Showers, and Thomas (2010).
8. Hinds and Cramton (2013).
9. Cross, Liedtka, and Weiss (2005).
10. Huckman and Staats (2013).
11. Rawson, Duncan, and Jones (2013).

Chapter 10

1. Gremler and Gwinner (2008).
2. Goffman (1959).
3. Deighton (1994).
4. Grove, Fisk, and Bitner (1992).
5. Grove, Fisk, and Bitner (1992).
6. Noe, Uysal, and Magnini (2010).
7. Magnini and Honeycutt (2005).
8. Hollman and Kleiner (1997).
9. Pease and Pease (2004).
10. Zaltman (1997).
11. DiMatteo, Taranta, Friedman, and Prince (1980).
12. Tickle-Degnen and Rosenthal (1990).
13. Bernieri, Gillis, Davis, and Grahe (1996).
14. Duggan and Parrott (2001).
15. Carnegie (1936), p. 63.
16. Magnini and Ford (2004).
17. Chiang and Jang (2008).
18. Gazzoli, Hancer, and Park (2010).
19. Lee, Kim, Perdue, and Magnini (2011).
20. Ciaramicoli and Ketcham (2000).
21. Netemeyer, Maxham, and Pullig (2005).

22. Bar-On (2007).
23. Lennick (2007).
24. Grandey (2000).
25. Totterdell and Holman (2003).
26. Heskett, Sasser, and Schlesinger (1997).
27. Hu, Martin, and Yeh (2002).
28. Puck, Kittler, and Wright (2008).
29. Burke and Hutchins (2007).
30. Burke and Hutchins (2007).
31. Baldwin and Ford (1988).
32. Lim and Morris (2006).
33. Rodriguez and Gregory (2005).
34. Facteau, Dobbins, Russell, Ladd, and Kudisch (1995).
35. Burke and Hutchins (2007).
36. Clarke (2002).
37. Gfeller, Lynn, and Pribble (1987).

Chapter 11

1. Brown (1989).
2. Lengnick-Hall (1996).
3. Berman, (2005).
4. Connellan (1996).
5. Bly (1993).

Chapter 12

1. Celente and Milton (1990a).
2. Celente and Milton (1990b).
3. Martin (2001).
4. Peters (2010).

Final Thought

1. Reisenzein (2000).
2. Ohmae (1999).
3. Fraering and Minor (2013).
4. Kapferer (2005).
5. Berman (2005).
6. Bitner, Booms, and Tetreault (1990).

7. Basadur, Graen, and Scandura (1986).

8. Woodman, Sawyer, and Griffin (1993).

9. Reisenzein (2000).

10. Smedslund (1990).

11. Peters and Austin (1985).

References

Agnihotri, R., A.A. Rapp, and C.B. Gabler. 2014. "Examining the Drivers and Performance Implications of Boundary Spanner Creativity." *Journal of Service Research* 17, no. 2, pp. 164–181.

Amabile, T. 1988. "A Model of Creativity and Innovation in Organizations." *Research in Organizational Behavior* 10, pp. 123–167.

Amabile, T. 1990. "Within You, Without You: The Social Psychology of Creativity and Beyond." In *Theories of Creativity*, eds. M.A. Runco, and R.S. Albert, pp. 61–91. Newbury Park, CA: Sage.

Axelrod, R. 1973. "Schema Theory: An Information Processing Model of Perception and Cognition." *The American Political Science Review* 67, no. 4, pp. 1248–1266.

Baldwin, T., and J. Ford. 1988. "Transfer of Training: A Review and Directions for Future Research." *Personnel Psychology* 41, pp. 63–105.

Bar-On, R. 2007. "How Important Is It to Educate People to Be Emotionally Intelligent, and Can It Be Done?" In *Educating People to Be Emotionally Intelligent*, eds. R. Bar-On, J. Maree, and M. Elias. Westport, CT: Praeger, pp. 1–35.

Barron, F., and D. Harrington, 1981. "Creativity, Intelligence, and Personality." *Annual Review of Psychology* 32, pp. 439–476.

Basadur M., G. Graen, and T. Scandura. 1986. "Training Effects on Attitudes Toward Divergent-Thinking Among Manufacturing Engineers." *Journal of Applied Psychology* 71, pp. 612–617.

Bateson, J. 2002. "Consumer Performance and Quality in Services." *Managing Service Quality* 12, no. 4, pp. 206–209.

Bawden, D. 2001. "Information Overload." *Library and Information Briefings*, London, UK: South Bank University.

Bawden, D., and L. Robinson. 2009. "The Dark Side of Information: Overload, Anxiety, and Other Paradoxes and Pathologies." *Journal of Information Science* 35, no. 2, pp. 180–191.

Berman, B. 2005. "How to Delight Your Customers." *California Management Review* 48, no. 1, pp. 129–151.

Berman, B. January, 2003. "Delight Moves Customer Responses to Next Level." *Business Wire*, p. 52.

Bernieri, F., J. Gillis, J. Davis, and J. Grahe. 1996. "Dyad Rapport and the Accuracy of Its Judgment Across Situations: A Lens Model Analysis." *Journal of Personality and Social Psychology* 71, no. 1, pp. 110–129.

Bies, R., and J. Moag. 1986. "Interactional Justice: Communication Criteria of Fairness." In *Research on Negotiations in Organizations* (Vol. 1), eds. R.J. Lewicki, B.H. Sheppard, and M.H. Bazerman. Greewich, CT: JAI, pp. 43–55.

Bitner, M., B. Booms, and L. Mohr. 1994. "Critical Service Encounters: The Employee's Viewpoint." *Journal of Marketing* 58, no. 10, pp. 95–106.

Bitner, M., B. Booms, and S. Tetreault. 1990. "The Service Encounter: Diagnosing Favorable and Unfavorable Incidents." *Journal of Marketing* 54, no. 1, pp. 71–84.

Blanchard, K., and S. Johnson. 1981. *The One Minute Manager*. New York, NY: The Berkley Publishing Company.

Bly, R. 1993. *Keeping Clients Satisfied*. Englewood Cliffs, NJ: Prentice Hall.

Boddy, C.R. 2007. "Projective Techniques in Taiwan and Asia-Pacific Market Research." *Qualitative Market Analysis: An International Journal* 10, no. 1, pp. 48–62.

Borgatti, S., and R. Cross. 2003. "A Relational View of Information Seeking and Learning in Social Networks." *Management Science* 49, no. 4, pp. 432–445.

Brown, A. 1989. *Customer Care Management*. Oxford, UK: Heinemann Professional.

Burke, L., and H. Hutchins. 2007. "Training Transfer: An Integrative Literature Review." *Human Resource Development Review* 6, no. 3, pp. 263–296.

Button, S., J. Mathieu, and D. Zajac 1996. "Goal Orientation in Organizational Research: A Conceptual and Empirical Foundation." *Organizational Behavior and Human Decision Processes* 67, no. 1, pp. 26–48.

Cabrera, A., W. Collins, and J. Salgado. 2006. "Determinants of Individual Engagement in Knowledge Sharing." *International Journal of Human Resource Management* 17, no. 2, pp. 245–264.

Carnegie, D. 1936. *How To Win Friends and Influence People*. London, UK: Hutchinson.

Celente, G., and T. Milton. 1990. *Trend Tracking*. New York, NY: Warner Books.

Chen, H., and N. Lim. 2013. "Should Managers Use Team-Based Contests?" *Management Science* 59, no. 12, pp. 2823–2836.

Chiang, C., and S. Jang. 2008. "The Antecedents and Consequences of Psychological Empowerment: The Case of Taiwan's Hotel Companies." *Journal of Hospitality and Tourism Research* 32, no. 1, pp. 40–61.

Ciaramicoli, A., and K. Ketcham. 2000. *The Power of Empathy*. New York, NY: The Penguin Group.

Clarke, N. 2002. "Job/Work Environment Factors Influencing Training Effectiveness Within a Human Service Agency: Some Indicative Support for Baldwin and Fords' Transfer Climate Construct." *International Journal of Training and Development* 63, pp. 146–162.

Connellan, T. 1996. *Inside the Magic Kingdom*. Austin, TX: Bard Press.

Cooper, E. 1991. "A Critique of Six Measures for Assessing Creativity." *Journal of Creative Behavior* 25, pp. 194–204.

Cropley, A.J. 2000. "Defining and Measuring Creativity: Are Creativity Tests Worth Using?" *Roeper Review* 23, no. 2, pp. 72–79.

Cross, R. et al. 2010. "The Collaborative Organization: How to Make Employee Networks Really Work." *MIT Sloan Management Review* 52, no. 1, pp. 83–97.

Cross, R., J. Liedtka, and L. Weiss. 2005. "A Practical Guide to Social Networks." *Harvard Business Review*, no. 3, pp. 1–10.

Crotts, J. and V. Magnini. 2011. "The Customer Delight Construct: Is Surprise Essential." *Annals of Tourism Research* 38, pp. 708–722.

Danziger, S., J. Levav, and L. Avnaim-Pesso. 2011. "Extraneous Factors in Judicial Decision." *Proceedings of the National Academy of Sciences* 108, pp. 6889–6892.

de Vries, R.E., B. van den Hoof, and J.A. Ridder. 2006. "Explaining Knowledge Sharing: The Role of Team Communication Styles, Job Satisfaction, and Performance Beliefs." *Communication Research* 33, no. 2, pp. 115–135.

Deal, T., and A. Kennedy. 1982. "Corporate Cultures: The Rites and Rituals on Corporate Life." Reading, MA: Addison-Wesley Publishing Company.

Deighton, J. 1994. "Managing Services When the Service Is a Performance." In *Service Quality*, eds. R.T. Rust, and R.L. Oliver. Thousand Oaks, CA: Sage Publications.

DiMatteo, M. et al. 1980. "Predicting Patient Satisfaction from Physicians' Nonverbal Communication Skills." *Medical Care* 18, no. 4, pp. 376–387.

Donnelly, J. 1992. *Close to the Customer*. Homewood, IL: Business One Irwin.

Drazin, R., M.A. Glynn, and R.K. Kazanjian. 1999. "Multilevel Theorizing and Creativity in Organizations: A Sense Making Perspective." *Academy of Management Review* 24, pp. 286–329.

Duggan, A., and R. Parrott. 2001. "Physicians' Nonverbal Rapport Building and Patients' Talk about the Subjective Component of Illness." *Human Communication Research* 27, no. 2, pp. 299–311.

Dweck, C. 1986. "Motivational Processes Affecting Learning." *American Psychologist* 41, pp. 1040–1048.

Dweck, C. 1989. "Motivation." In *Foundations for a Psychology of Education*, eds. A. Lesgold, and R. Glaser. Hillsdale, NJ: Earlbaum.

Dweck, C., and E. Leggett. 1988. "A Social-Cognitive Approach to Motivation and Personality." *Psychological Review* 95, pp. 256–273.

Facteau, J. et al. 1995. "The Influence of General Perceptions of the Training Environment on Pre-Training Motivation and Perceived Training Transfer." *Journal of Management* 21, pp. 1–25.

Fisher, R.J. 1993. "Social Desirability Bias and the Validity of Indirect Questioning." *Journal of Consumer Research* 20, no. 2, pp. 303–315.

Fraering, M., and M. Minor. 2013. "Beyond Loyalty: Customer Satisfaction, Loyalty, and Fortitude." *Journal of Services Marketing* 27, no. 4, pp. 334–344.

Gazzoli, G., M. Hancer, and Y. Park. 2010. "The Role and Effect of Job Satisfaction and Empowerment on Customers' Perception of Service Quality: A Study in the Restaurant Industry." *Journal of Hospitality and Tourism Research* 34, no. 1, pp. 56–77.

Lee, G. et al. 2011. "Time-Varying Effects of Empowerment on Job Satisfaction for Customer-Contact Versus Non-Customer-Contact Groups." *Proceeding of the 16th Annual Graduate Student Research Conference in Hospitality and Tourism.*

Gfeller, J., S. Lynn, and W. Pribble. 1987. "Enhancing Hypnotic Susceptibility: Interpersonal and Rapport Factors." *Journal of Personality and Social Psychology* 25, no. 3, pp. 586–595.

Gladwell, M. 2008. *Outliers.* New York, NY: Backbay Books.

Goffman, E. 1959. *The Presentation of Self in Everyday Life.* Garden City, NY: Doubleday.

Gonzalez, V., and G. Mark. 2004. "Constant, Constant, Multi-Tasking Craziness: Managing Multiple Working Spheres." In *Proceedings of the CHI'04,* ACM Press.

Gounaris, S., and A. Boukis. 2013. "The Role of Employee Satisfaction in Strengthening Customer Repurchase Intentions." *Journal of Services Marketing* 27, no. 4, pp. 322–333.

Grandey, A. 2000. "Emotion Regulation in the Workplace: A New Way to Conceptualize Emotional Labor." *Journal of Occupational Health Psychology* 5, pp. 95–110.

Grant, A. 2013. *Give and Take: A Revolutionary Approach to Success.* New York, NY: Viking.

Gremler, D.D., and K.P. Gwinner. 2008. "Rapport-Building Behaviors Used by Retail Employees." *Journal of Retailing* 84, no. 3, 308–324.

Gronroos, C., and P. Voima. 2013. "Critical Service Logic: Making Sense of Value Creation and Co-Creation." *Journal of the Academy of Marketing Science* 41, pp. 133–150.

Grove, S., R. Fisk., and M. Bitner. 1992. "Dramatizing the Service Experience: A Managerial Approach." In *Advances in Services Marketing and Management.* Greenwich, CT: JAI Press.

Hansen, M., M. Mors, and B. Lovas 2005. "Knowledge Sharing in Organizations: Multiple Networks, Multiple Phases." *Academy of Management Journal* 48, no. 5, pp. 776–793.

Hargadon, A. 1998. "Firms as Knowledge Brokers: Lessons in Pursuing Continuous Innovation." *California Management Review* 40, no. 3, pp. 209–227.

Hargadon, A.B., and R.I. Sutton. 1997. "Technology Brokering and Innovation in a Product Development Firm." *Administrative Science Quarterly* 42, pp. 716–749.

Hargadon, A.B., and R.I. Sutton. May–June, 2000. "Building the Innovation Factory." *Harvard Business Review* 78, no. 3, pp. 157–166.

Hart, C., J. Heskett, and E. Sasser. 1990. "The Profitable Art of Service Recovery." *Harvard Business Review* 68, no. 7–8, pp. 148–156.

Heskett, J.L., E.W. Sasser, and L.A. Schlesinger. 1997. *The Service Profit Chain*. New York, NY: The Free Press.

Hewlett, S., M. Marshall, and L. Sherbin. December, 2013. "How Diversity Can Drive Innovation." *Harvard Business Review*.

Hinds, P., and C. Cramton. 2013. "Situated Coworker Familiarity: How Site Visits Transform Relationships Among Distributed Workers." *Organization Science* 25, no. 3, pp. 794–814.

Ho, S. 2013. "Making Magic: Creating Next-Level Disney Experiences." *Virginia Tech Business Magazine*, Fall edition, pp. 4–7.

Hoevemeyer, V. 2005. *High-Impact Interview Questions: 701 Behavior-Based Questions to Find the Right Person for Every Job*. New York, NY: Amacon Books.

Hollman, W., and B. Kleiner. 1997: "Establishing Rapport: The Secret Business Tool." *Managing Service Quality* 7, no. 4, pp. 194–197.

"Jokes and Riddles for Kids." 2013. *Enchanted Learning*. http://www.enchantedlearning.com/jokes/ (October 30, 2013).

Hu, W., L. Martin, and J. Yeh. 2002. "Cross-Cultural Impact and Learning Needs For Expatriate Hotel Employees in Taiwan's Lodging Industry." *Journal of Human Resources in Hospitality and Tourism* 1, pp. 31–45.

Huckman, R., and B. Staats. December, 2013. "The Hidden Benefits of Keeping Teams Intact." *Harvard Business Review* 91, no. 12, 27–29..

Kahneman, D. 2011. *Thinking Fast and Slow*. New York, NY: Farrar, Straus, and Giroux.

Kapferer, J. 2005. "The Roots of Brand Loyalty Decline: An International Comparison." *Ivey Business Journal* 69, no. 4, pp. 1–6.

Kaufman, R. 2012. *Uplifting Service*. New York, NY: Evolve Publishing.

Kim, M., and A. Mattila. 2013. "Does a Surprise Strategy Need Words? The Effect of Explanations for a Surprise Strategy on Customer Delight and Expectations." *Journal of Services Marketing* 27, no. 5, pp. 361–370.

Kohli, A., T. Shervani, and G. Challagalla, G. 1998. "Learning and Performance Orientation of Salespeople: The Role of Supervisors." *Journal of Marketing Research* 35, no. 2, pp. 263–274.

Leavy, B. 2005. "A Leader's Guide to Creating an Innovation Culture." *Strategy and Leadership* 33, no. 4, pp. 38–45.

Lengnick-Hall, C. 1996. "Customer Contributions to Quality: A Different View of the Customer-Oriented Firm." *Academy of Management Executive* 21, no. 3, pp. 791–824.

Lennick, D. 2007. "Emotional Competence Development and the Bottom Line: Lessons from American Express Financial Advisors." In *Educating People to be Emotionally Intelligent*, eds. R. Bar-On, J. Maree, M. Elias. Westport, CT: Praeger, pp. 199–210.

Lim, D., and M. Morris. 2006. "Influence of Trainee Characteristics, Instructional Satisfaction, and Organizational Climate on Perceived Learning and Training Transfer." *Human Resource Development Quarterly* 17, pp. 85–115.

Lind, E., R. Kanfer, and C. Early. 1988. *The Sociology Psychology of Procedural Justice*. New York, NY: Plenum.

Magnini, V., and E. Honeycutt. 2005 "Face Recognition and Name Recall: Training Implications for the Hospitality Industry." *Cornell Hospitality Quarterly* 46, no. 1, pp. 69–78.

Magnini, V., and J. Ford. 2004. "Service Failure Recovery in China." *International Journal of Contemporary Hospitality Management* 16, no. 5, pp. 279–286.

Magnini, V., J. Crotts, and A. Zehrer. 2011. "Understanding Customer Delight: An Application of Travel Blog Analysis." *Journal of Travel Research* 50, no. 5, pp. 535–545.

Magnini, V., J. Ford, E. Markowski, and E. Honeycutt, Jr. 2007. "The Service Recovery Paradox: Justifiable Theory or Smoldering Myth." *Journal of Services Marketing* 21, no. 3, pp. 213–225.

Magnini, V.P., and E.D. Honeycutt, Jr. 2003. "Learning Orientation and the Hotel Expatriate Manager Experience." *International Journal of Hospitality Management* 22, pp. 267–280.

Malakate, A., C. Andriopoulos, and M. Gotsi. 2007. "Assessing Job Candidate's Creativity: Propositions and Future Research Directions." *Creativity and Innovation Management* 16, no. 3, pp. 307–316.

"Marketing: Less Guff, More Puff." 2013. *The Economist*. www.economist.com/news/business, (May 27, 2014).

Martin, R. 2001. "Humor, Laughter, and Physical Health: Methodological Issues and Research Findings." *Psychological Bulletin* 127, no. 4, pp. 504–519.

Mayer, J., and P. Salovey, P. 1997. What is Emotional Intelligence? In *Emotional Development and Emotional Intelligence: Educational Implications*, eds. P. Salovey, and D. Slutyer. New York, NY: Basic Books, pp. 3–31.

Meyer, W. 1997. "Towards a Process Analysis of Emotions: The Case of Surprise." *Motivation and Emotion* 21, pp. 251–274.

Michelli, J. 2008. *The New Gold Standard*. New York, NY: McGraw Hill.

Netemeyer, R., J. Maxham, III., and C. Pullig. 2005. "Conflicts in the Work-Family Interface: Links to Job Stress, Customer Service Employee Performance, and Customer Repurchase Intention." *Journal of Marketing* 69, no. 2, pp. 130–143.

Noe, F., M. Uysal, and V. Magnini. 2010. *Tourist Customer Satisfaction: An Encounter Approach*. London, UK: Routledge.

Nunes, J., and X. Dreze. 2006. "The Endowed Progress Effect: How Artificial Advancement Increases Effort." *Journal of Consumer Research* 32, no. 4, pp. 504–512.

Ohmae, K. 1999. *The Borderless World: Power and Strategy in the Interlinked Economy*. 2nd ed. New York, NY: Harper Collins.

Oldham, G.R., and A. Cummings. 1996. "Employee Creativity: Personal and Contextual Factors at Work." *Academy of Management Journal* 39, pp. 607–634.

Oliver, R. 1980. "A Cognitive Model of the Antecedents and Consequences of Satisfaction Decisions." *Journal of Marketing Research* 17, pp. 460–469.

Oulasvirta, A. 2005. "The Fragmentation of Attention in Mobile Interaction, and What to Do with It." *Interactions* 12, no. 6, pp. 16–18.

Palmer, A, R. Beggs, and C. Keown-McMullan 2000. "Equity and Repurchase Intent Following Service Failure." *Journal of Services Marketing* 14, no. 6, pp. 513–526.

Pascoe, C., T. Ali, and L. Warne. 2002. "Yet Another Role for Job Satisfaction and Work Motivation—Enabler of Knowledge Creation and Knowledge Sharing." *Proceedings of the Informing Science + IT Education Conference*, pp. 1239–1248.

Pease, A., and B. Pease. 2004. *The Definitive Book of Body Language*. New York, NY: Bantam Dell.

Perry-Smith, J., and C. Shalley. 2003. "The Social Side of Creativity: A Static and Dynamic Social Network Perspective." *Academy of Management Review* 28, no. 1, pp. 89–106.

Peteraf, M. 1993. "The Cornerstones of Competitive Advantage: A Resource-Based View." *Strategic Management Journal* 14, no. 3, pp. 179–191.

Peters, T. 2010. "The Little Big Things: 163 Ways to Pursue Excellence." New York, NY: Harper Business.

Peters, T., and N. Austin. 1985. *A Passion for Excellence*. New York, NY: Warner Books.

Pine, J. II, and J. Gilmore. July-August, 1998. "Welcome to the Experience Economy." *Harvard Business Review*, pp. 97–105.

Porter, G., and J. Tansky. 1999. "Expatriate Success May Depend on a 'Learning Orientation': Considerations for Selection and Training." *Human Resource Management* 38, no. 1, pp. 47–60.

Puck, J.F., M.G. Kittler, and C. Wright. 2008. "Does It Really Work? Re-Assessing the Impact of Pre-Departure Cross-Cultural Training on Expatriate Adjustment." *International Journal of Human Resource Management* 19, pp. 2182–2197.

Ramdas, K., E. Teisberg, and A. Tucker. December, 2012. "Four Ways to Reinvent Service Delivery." *Harvard Business Review*, pp. 99–106.

Rawson, A., E. Duncan, and C. Jones. 2013. "The Truth about Customer Experience." *Harvard Business Review* 91, no. 9, 90–98.

Reisenzein, R. 2000. "The Subjective Experience of Surprise." In *The Message Within*, eds. H. Bless., and J. Forgas. Philadelphia, PA: Psychology Press.

Rodriguez, C., and S. Gregory. 2005. "Qualitative Study of Transfer of Training of Student Employees in a Service Industry." *Journal of Hospitality and Tourism Research* 29, pp. 42–66.

Roizen, M., and M. Oz. 2005. *You: The Owner's Manual.* New York, NY: Harper Collins.

Rothenberg, A. 1996. "The Janusian Process in Scientific Discovery." *Creativity Research Journal* 9, pp. 207–232.

Rumbo, J. 2002. "Consumer Resistance in a World of Advertising Clutter: The Case of Adbusters." *Psychology and Marketing* 19, no. 2, pp. 127–148.

Salovey, P., and J. Mayer. 1990. "Emotional Intelligence." *Imagination, Cognition, and Personality* 9, no. 3, pp. 185–211.

Sanborn, M. 2004. *The Fred Factor.* New York, NY: Doubleday.

Simonton, D.K. 2000. "Creativity: Cognitive, Personal, Developmental and Social Aspects." *American Psychologist* 55, pp. 151–158.

Smedslund, J. 1990. "Psychology and Psychologic: Characterization of the Difference." *In Everyday Understanding: Social and Scientific Implications* (Vol. 29, pp. 45–63), eds. K. Gergen, and G. Semin. London, UK: Sage.

Smith, R., and M. Houston 1985. "A Psychometric Assessment of Measures of Scripts in Consumer Memory." *Journal of Consumer Research* 12, no. 2, pp. 214–224.

Stroop, J. 1935. "Studies of Interference in Serial Verbal Reactions." *Journal of Experimental Psychology* 18, no. 6, pp. 643–662.

Tickle-Degnen, L., and R. Rosenthal. 1990. "The Nature of Rapport and Nonverbal Correlates." *Psychological Inquiry* 1, no. 4, pp. 285–293.

Tisch, J., and K. Weber. 2007. *Chocolates on the Pillow Aren't Enough.* Hoboken, NJ: John Wiley and Sons.

Totterdell, P., and D. Holman. 2003. "Emotion Regulation in Customer Service Roles: Testing a Model of Emotional Labor." *Journal of Occupational Health Psychology* 8, no. 1, pp. 55–73.

VandeWalle, D. 2001. "Why Wanting to Look Successful Doesn't Always Lead to Success." *Organizational Dynamics* 30, no. 2, pp. 162–171.

VandeWalle, D, et al. 1999. "The Influence of Goal Orientation and Self-Regulation on Sales Performance: A Longitudinal Field Study." *Journal of Applied Psychology* 84, no. 2, pp. 249–259.

Wang, Y., and S. Nicholas. 2005. "Knowledge Transfer, Knowledge Replication, and Learning in Non-Equity Alliances: Operating Contractual Joint Ventures in China." *Management International Review* 45, no. 1, pp. 99–118.

Wernerfelt, B. 1984. "A Resource-Based View of the Firm." *Strategic Management Journal* 5, no. 2, pp. 171–180.

Woodman, R., J. Sawyer, and R. Griffin. 1993. "Toward a Theory of Organizational Creativity." *Academy of Management Review* 18, no. 2, pp. 293–321.

Zaltman, G. 1997. "Rethinking Marketing Research: Putting People Back In." *Journal of Marketing Research* 34, no. 4, pp. 424–437.

Zeithaml, V., M. Bitner, and D. Gremler. 2006. *Services Marketing: Integrating Customer Focus Across the Firm.* Boston, MA: McGraw-Hill Irwin.

Index

www.ingramcontent.com/pod-product-compliance
Lightning Source LLC
Chambersburg PA
CBHW062024200326
41519CB00017B/4918